T5-AQR-227

20°

990B

Strategy
of
Therapy

Strategy of Therapy

Toward the Engineering of Social Growth

By

GEORGE T. TATE, Ph.D.

*Chief Psychologist, Veterans Administration
Hospital, Alexandria, Louisiana*

SPRINGER PUBLISHING COMPANY, Inc., NEW YORK

This book is respectfully dedicated to
the memory of my father

HAYNES MILTON TATE

who taught me my ABC's, and to value them and
the inviolable dignity of every person, and to
everyone in history, in our day and yet to appear
whose lives express this value.

Copyright © 1967

SPRINGER PUBLISHING COMPANY, INC.
200 Park Avenue South, New York, New York

Library of Congress Catalog Card No.: 67-27711

Composition by Topel Typographic Corp.
Printed in U.S.A.

Foreword

Group psychotherapy in this country has had a long and, until fairly recently, a not overly honored existence. Most practitioners have viewed group therapy as a useful ancillary technique or a "faut de mieux" procedure. What clearly emerges from George Tate's book is that for many, if not most, problems of behavior, working in a group setting is the treatment procedure of *choice*. He presents a meaningful framework into which the therapist can fit his techniques so that he is not merely filling up time but has a purpose for whatever he says and does in the group. The framework is also one into which can be fitted the specific behaviors of the patients which the therapist choses to work with, emphasize, or reinforce.

It may be argued that all therapists work from a theoretical frame of reference which, implicitly or explicitly, determines their behavior. Tate's framework, with its emphasis on the salient and observable behaviors of the individual, belongs most naturally within the broad category of "behavioral" approaches which can be contrasted with the more traditional "psychodynamic" procedures. Tate is concerned with the end product of early influences on the individual, namely his *current* behavior. His formulation of behavior moves him far afield from the "disease" model involving sick and sickening behavior; it moves him in the direction of conceptualizing the patient's problems in social terms. Tate is then very explicit about the therapist's social responsibilities that he has by virtue of being cast in the role of leading a group of "responsible" individuals.

Are Tate's formulations new or do they represent a restatement of views commonly held? Certainly there is almost nothing new under the sun. However, Tate not only brings a *unique* formulation to our attention, but in every detail he carefully

v

cites the origin of his ideas. His knowledge of the literature in this area is extensive, and he demonstrates throughout the book what concepts he is using, from whose formulations he deviates, and how. This kind of synthesis represents an important and useful contribution. I particularly like the way in which Tate, in each chapter, presents his theoretical views and follows these with a review of the pertinent literature from which his ideas were abstracted.

Tate's conceptualization of the two therapeutic processes, contrasting and substituting, subsumes most of the therapeutic techniques now in current practice. This is summarized in Chapter III as follows: "The aim of contrasting, then, is to improve understanding, which the client can then use to improve his behavior. The aim of substituting is to improve his behavior but not his understanding. Contrasting is a progressive alteration of the client's verbal model of the nature of the relationship, which assists the client in gaining control of the distortions he brings into his relationships. Therapeutic gain through contrasting is mediated by understanding: through substituting, it is direct and unmediated."

This is a very useful distinction between the goals and purposes of "insight" therapy and those of behavior therapy. Tate would carefully interweave these two broad techniques in such a way as to have the best of both worlds. Can this be done or is he trying to do the impossible? We might argue that there is one process in psychotherapy that is more generic than either substituting or contrasting. We would label this process as "social influence." The goal of psychotherapy is to change patient behavior by manipulation of social influence. The means of carrying out this goal is by the planned utilization of the therapist's behavior to affect his client's responses. "Substituting" is clearly within this broad framework but is "contrasting," the use of "insight," also part of this broader generic process? As Tate formulates it, it definitely is, since it has the two characteristics that are necessary for procedures to be subsumed as part of social or behavior influence: it involves the *systematic* and the *contingent* use of the therapist's behavior (in the group situation), primarily his verbalizations, to institute a specified change in the patient's behavior.

Certainly Tate is aware of the social implications of an approach involving "substituting" as he describes it. Such a procedure moves over into involvement with a total institution and with the community when appropriate. Substituting involves a greater control over the individual environment than contrasting procedures do. I particularly like the term substituting because it so ably captures what is involved in the "substitution" of one behavior for another, of a socially *adaptive* behavior for a socially *maladaptive* one. It also emphasizes the point that it is not enough to extinguish or to eliminate a behavior; since a human being is always doing something, a new, more desirable, behavior must be substituted. In order to carry out both goals, that of contrasting and that of substituting, specific techniques must be used, i.e., the therapist's behavior must be planned and deliberate. In this context we would include such "techniques" as nondirective reflection, psychoanalytic interpretation, reciprocal inhibition, operant conditioning, role taking, and the use of hypnotic procedures.

Tate does more than present a theoretical or developmental framework. He spells out in careful, clear terms the behavior to be expected of the therapist in each phase of group therapy. He hypothesizes as to the behavior that may be expected of the client in different phases of therapy, and how the therapist should react to the behavior of clients. He offers illustrations for the different types of behavior that may be anticipated as a function of the different social settings of the groups in therapy. At some points so clearly does Tate spell out some of the alternatives available to the therapist that the reader vividly supplies his own specific behaviors as if he were in the actual group situation.

Yet there is one more thing. The book cries out for a sequel. What kind of data would Tate's framework engender? One can have a lot of fun speculating but data speak loudly, and Tate's orientation and description should lend themselves to application in a controlled research context.

What does the book tell us about the author? He is a kindly humanitarian who stops just short of being a tough-minded behavior therapist. He blends the most meaningful qualities of both and demonstrates that the two are not incompatible but are, in fact, the two sides of the same proverbial coin. Both of these qualities, the warmth and affection for his fellow men and the scientific detachment of the effective modifier of behavior, are the ingredients necessary to successful psychotherapy. Tate is exciting in finally bringing together those elements of the therapist that belong together, and that enable him to focus on the only purpose of the psychotherapeutic situation: to change the client's problem behavior.

LEONARD KRASNER
Stony Brook, New York

Preface

The subject matter of this book concerns individuals, communities and nations. It touches on a basic human task, long ago assigned to the family: the progressive and orderly change of infant into adult. The book offers a conceptual framework for understanding the growth process, and a systematic approach to the behavioral problem that results when things go wrong in the family's management of its assignment.

The principle evolves from theoretical considerations that those who would stimulate growth must define their relationship to the growing child in a way to make room for his growth. The book represents the best formulation I can make from my own experience. For example, the sensitivity to the influence of organizational structure on professional practice derives from my having practiced psychology in a number of organizational settings; the program of therapeutic intervention in the psychotic deviation draws most heavily on my five years of participation in the group therapy program at the Veterans Administration hospital at Gulfport. I believe that my academic and practical experience and a lifetime of effort to understand the "strategy of therapy" entitles me to speak—at least tentatively and hypothetically. The determination of the status of my ideas belongs to the community of social scientists to whom the book is especially addressed.

The ideas developed here should aid the therapist who has supervisory responsibilities. The book provides him with a system of interlocking terms which he can use to express his evaluation of the therapeutic situation. The book should assist students of therapy in grasping the kinds of problems they must face and solve in order to function effectively as therapists.

Since the book is focused on the strategic level and does not go into details of technique, it permits a presentation of the broad

outlines of therapy in descriptive language that is suitable for anyone seriously interested in the subject. I have in mind the many
people who do not practice therapy but who participate in admin-
istrative and professional activities that directly or indirectly influence therapy, such as legislators, judges, administrators of
programs that include therapy or behavioral correction, teachers,
nurses, non-psychiatric physicians, and social workers. Since the
objectives of therapy are clearly defined, the book will also assist
those who educate the public about mental health matters.

The book follows a simple, natural order. Chapter I deals
with the changing features of behavior between infancy and
adulthood—when things go right. Chapter II describes how things
go wrong and what happens when they do. Chapters III, IV and
V present the theoretical and practical considerations that facilitate the technical management of the corrective process. Chapters
VI through IX develop a program of therapeutic intervention for
the psychotic deviation, based on the strategic objectives defined
in the first five chapters. Chapter VI deals with initial arrangements; Chapters VII, VIII and IX describe the changes of the
therapist's participation that parallel the growth of the client. In
order to avoid interrupting the overall system, I have placed all
reference to the literature at the end of each chapter. I develop
what I have to say first and then offer a view of it in the perspective of the literature. The book draws on my total experience;
all the many people who have influenced me have a part in this
book. In particular, I would like to express my gratitude to the
Veterans Administration for the opportunities to study and practice psychology it has given me; to thank the students and members of the staff at Gulfport who permitted me to observe their
therapy sessions and especially those who listened to my first,
generally unsuccessful effort to articulate the point of view presented in this book; to thank A. J. Roberts, M.D., whose firm
support was essential to the group therapy program at Gulfport.
Full responsibility for the book is of course mine and no one
else's. I would like to give very special thanks to Miss Patricia
Orrok and her staff at the Central Louisiana State Hospital Medical Library of Pineville, Louisiana, and to Miss Mildred Haw-

thorn and her staff at the library of the VA Hospital, Alexandria, Louisiana, for excellent library assistance. Finally, I would like to thank my wife Bibby and my daughter Vivian for their tolerance of the interruption of our family life by the preparation of the book.

May 1967   GEORGE T. TATE
Alexandria, Louisiana

Contents

Developmental Process

Between birth and death a person demonstrates and goes through an infinite number of changes in his emotional life. Under adequate conditions of growth, one phase flows into the next phase. There is a natural progression of the emotional life: an earlier phase prepares for and finds fulfillment in the next phase. So gradual and orderly are the changes that the person has no difficulty in recognizing the continuity of himself through the entirety of his life cycle.

Each person has an individual developmental sequence that is different in the rate in which various features form and change. This individual developmental sequence is dependent upon the peculiarity and specificity of experience, especially and predominantly, interpersonal experience. An individual developmental sequence may fail to flow into the next phase either because of a lack of certain experiences or because of the occurrence of certain experiences, or an individual may begin to show behaviorial characteristics of a later phase and then revert to the kind of behavior he showed at an earlier time.

The orderly sequence of changes which occur as the person moves from birth to maturity is called growth. The falling back to an earlier pattern of behavior is called retreat. A lingering in a particular phase for a longer time than is required by biological limitation is called stagnation. Change and movement according to the developmental sequence are natural and desirable. A failure to grow is undesirable and abnormal. A small change is made in the movement from one "phase" to the next; a large change, to the point of major re-orientation, is reflected in movement from one "stage" to the next. The totality of behaviorial features at a given moment in his developmental sequence is called the emotional life of the person.

Although each person's developmental sequence is uniquely his own, from study and observation of many growth patterns, an expected or theoretical developmental scale can be constructed of the common features. The developmental scale summarizes the empirically-determined invariant sequence of growth. A particular feature of emotional life, such as awareness of self, may be described in terms of its progressive modification, as one moves up the developmental scale. The description may give, on the other hand, the usual or expected emotional life at a particular point on the developmental scale. Both kinds of descriptions are needed. Such a model of developmental scale would permit a rating of the relative maturity of the emotional life shown by an individual. Two descriptions at different points in time would permit judgment of whether the individual has grown, retreated, or stagnated. Such a model would assume " (under) adequate conditions of growth." It would reflect what an individual's emotional life would be like, if his experiences have supported and not blocked his growth.

The following description of some of the major features of emotional life during six developmental stages will serve to illustrate and permit discussion of the concept of developmental scale. The description of the stages is not intended to be either exhaustive or definitive. Special emphasis is given to those features of emotional life that may be observed or inferred during the course of therapy. Since the developmental scale is a model of emotional growth, deviations are not considered.

Stages of development

Early infancy. In earliest infancy attention is not focused on any particular object; behavior is random, unstructured, unordered and very loosely related to situation; reaction is total, undifferentiated. In early infancy this feature changes into special attention to bright lights and moving objects. There is a growing tendency to distribute attention differentially upon the various stimuli. Still later in the sequence there is evidence of preferential reactions to objects; that is, an organization of behavior related to a specific situation. The first object to gain such preferential status is the nourishing object. At first, preferential reactions tend to be gross, either total pleasure or total misery. The infant has negligible control over whether objects he likes or objects he dislikes will come into contact with him. He cries when he is miserable, which brings someone to take care of his needs. Gradually, with repetition of the experience of mother, father, sister, nurse and so on coming and giving relief, he develops a characteristic pattern of relating to others, which is the major part of his emotional life. The shaping of the pattern depends both on what those who care for him do and how he responds. During the first year of life the infant is given unqualified love and acceptance. He is not good or bad depending on what he does. He is always good, worthy and lovable. His needs are attended to quickly, with no more effort on his part than to make it known through crying that he needs something. Crying, followed by attention from the mother, followed by relief and security, are the dominant emotional events of an infant's life. The infant develops an attachment to and dependence on the mother to the point that very early in the life sequence he will prefer physical discomforts in her presence and with soothing sounds from her to physical comfort in her absence. The relationship of the infant to the mother overshadows all others. The infant may give passing attention to and receive passing pleasure from contacts with other people but these relationships compared to that with the mother are like stars compared to the sun. When the mother has reached such dominant significance in the emotional life of the infant, the stage of early infancy ends.

Late infancy. The mother uses her dominance and power in the emotional life of the infant to encourage his contacts with other people and things. During infancy she proudly displays him to family and friends. She expresses her delight that he does not go to sleep on Aunt Martha and that he smiles at Uncle John. She may carry on a conversation with others for him as if she were the infant. She turns him around and holds him in a position facing other people. If other people hold him, she speaks soothingly to the child of his safety. With the beginning of speech, she will instruct him to say specific words in his contacts with others. Still later when he is talking well, she will instruct him to use certain words in greeting and leave-taking and she will encourage the continuity of his relationships. "Tell Bobby you had a good time," she says. "Tell him to come to see you soon." Only gradually do the child's relationships to other people develop stability and independence from his relationship to the mother. For several years their continuity and growth is dependent upon the mother's support and encouragement.

Even with his mother's careful support of his relationships to children his age, he has little investment in peer relationships. They are usually broken without serious emotional repercussions. Judgments of his peers have little effect on him, but how his mother feels about him is of life and death significance. It is the judgments of the mother that make up reality. There is no appeal from them, no higher authority to which he may go. In order to gain and retain her approval, he gives up his highly individual way of life and shapes his behavior to conform more nearly to the mother's expectations of him.

In the second year of life there is a beginning of pressure on the child to do some things and not to do other things. The reactions toward him change from total approval to a mixture of approval and disapproval; evaluations change from "always good" to "sometimes good" and "sometimes bad." What he does may please or may upset the mother. At first he experiences these expectations and evaluations of him as alien and imposed from without. It is only in late childhood that he begins to demonstrate the influence of these rules in the quality of his behavior in a smooth, natural way; the rules are a part of himself. There is no suggestion of burden or effort in his manner. He acts in accordance with the rules automatically. There is, however, a midway point between these extremes of outside and inside: he observes the rules when he aims to please the person who is making them. The child does his homework if he likes a teacher. If he falls out with the one making the rules, he is perfectly free to disobey or disregard those rules. The applicability of the rules is dependent upon the continued good relationship with the person in authority. There are many variations along this continuum, and these can be appreciated by careful description of the individual case.

With the appearance of expectations for his conduct from the mother, there is the beginning of the problem for the child of maintaining his self-esteem. When behavior conflicts with expectation, one must offer justification, must excuse or explain the discrepancy. The mother will explain and excuse the child's behavior to the child and she will show preferential reactions to the excuses and explanations that he offers. She will thus have a decisive effect in determining the kinds of excuses and explanations that will become a characteristic part of the infant's behavior.

There is a growing awareness of self and of the differences between self and not-self. This is shown by increasingly discriminating behavior and the emergence of self-criticism. The self is a concept derived from consistencies of experience. It is derived from such experiences as noting the difference between a sensation when parts of his body are moved, pinched or hit and the experience when a pillow is moved, pinched or hit. The experience of difference from the mother is much more vivid when he resists her than when he complies with her demands. For this reason the infant resists the mother, not because of a conflict of goals but for the experience of his being different. It is the beginning of the recognition of power or control of one's self. Under optimal conditions there would be freedom to develop an accurate concept of the self, a concept that would take into account the totality of experience. Never do such conditions exist. There is inevitably some distortion of the concept of self in order to facilitate the activities of excusing and explaining, which reaches destructive proportions in the neurotic deviation described in Chapter II. With tenuous peer relationships, a self differentiated from not-self, and techniques for maintaining self-respect in a system of merit rather than inherent worth, late infancy ends.

Childhood. Starting school is a momentous event. It greatly increases the contact with and relative influence of the community. If the mother permits the child the freedom to participate fully in this experience, it can correct many deficiencies and limitations of experience up to this time. Until the beginning of school, there is little experience except with home and family. Consequently, the way the child relates himself to the world is largely derived from these restricted and comparatively narrow experiences. Under the impact of broader and closer contact with the community, the child's interpersonal pattern undergoes significant modification (unless this is blocked by the nature of the relationship to the mother).

The child is brought into contact with a host of people who have diverse and limited kinds of authority over him. The concept of total and absolute authority gives way to that of a hierarchy of authority. One person in authority takes him to school and may require him to sit down or stand up or get off the bus or wait about getting off but has no authority over what will be studied that day. Another authority tells him when he may play and when he must study, when he may recite and when he must remain quiet. He learns that the teacher's authority is appealable, both to his parents and to the principal. The old problem of excusing and explaining takes on new attributes in his relationship to a host of authorities. The problem had been one of maintaining his status with the mother; it is now the problem of maintaining status with the community. He discovers that the excuses and explanations that had the finest and purest validity with the mother are degraded and invalidated by some or many of these authorities. He must learn a new system of excuses and explanations in his relationships with the community. It is this new learning that makes a corrective experience for the limitations of the home.

Childhood is a stage of detailed elaboration of the infantile discovery of difference from other people. A clear and definite distinction is made in the interpersonal environment of the school between boys and girls. The distinction includes not only what one *is* but also what one *does*. Boys are expected to be rowdy, rambunctious, difficult to control, definitely less concerned about tidiness and manners. Girls are expected to be less energetic, neat, polite, sociable and athletically weaker. It is the time of the beginning of the question of one's adequacy as a boy and man or as a girl and woman.

In the school the child learns that he and his family are different from his schoolmates and teachers. He may come home in tears upon hearing in uncomplimentary terms that he is a democrat or socialist; Protestant or Buddhist; a spoiled rich brat or poor white trash. In the relationship with the mother, he has never been evaluated in these terms. Attributes that were of sacred status in infancy may be blasphemous in the interpersonal environment of the school. It is a time of coming to terms that he can live with about his being different from others. It is an opportunity to lay the groundwork for the development of a respect and admiration for the differentness of others.

At the same time he is learning of his uniqueness, there are new opportunities for cooperation and sharing. With the emergence of the self, there is a fascination in resistance and possession. As the self becomes more stable, there is a readiness for experiences that will expand the self through cooperation and sharing. It is the very beginning of participation in group goals and activities. If the class sings a song well, the child feels complimented and expanded. If the class sings poorly, the child feels criticized and smaller. He discovers that through cooperation and sharing he can overcome many of his limitations as an individual. If he contributes his ball, and others provide a bat and mitts and a place to play, then he can enjoy participating in a ball game. He and his ball alone cannot provide such experience. He is occupied a great deal of the time in learning and developing rules to guide this new kind of relationship to peers. For playing and having a good time, peers are useful and assist in fulfillment. What they say may be interesting and funny, but it is not usually serious; it is not reality. The judgments of peers are still of little importance and are readily dismissed if they conflict with those of adults.

In a matter of a few years, his experience in school life leads to disciplined behavior. He learns to mold and shape his behavior according to certain rules and to maintain a direction over an extended period of time, perhaps several days or weeks, in the pursuit of an objective. He learns to perform on command. He exercises an ever-increasing control over his own behavior.

Pre-adolescence. During the childhood years the school separates the children according to sex. As the child moves into the period of three to five years before puberty, he separates himself according to sex; the boys most definitely do this but to a lesser extent the girls also. Pre-adolescence is a period of elaborating the difference in sex discovered in childhood. As a member of a group of his own sex the child participates in the development of a very definite set of standards which are applicable to that group and to the relationships of the group to other similar organizations. The standards are not an effort to remake or reshape the adult world. It is the first appearance of a peer organization that is not managed by the adults. Peer judgments may be of great importance if made by his own group or may be of no significance if made by an alien or opposing group. The opposite sex is ignored in the building of a culture that is wholly suited to his own needs. The opposite sex during this developmental stage is as alien as are creatures from another planet, and there is little motivation to discover. what these alien creatures are like. It is a time of elaborating those attributes of his own sex that are not associated with amiable contact and cooperation with the opposite sex.

The pre-adolescent image of what a man is like is grossly distorted and inadequate. Even so, it is a developmental form that is modified during adolescence to become a mature conception of masculinity in adulthood. The heroes of this all-man culture are soldiers, pirates, and Superman. Masculinity takes on heroic qualities. He may rescue the fair sex to dramatize the heroism but he does not linger long to associate with her. It is a heroism for the sake of heroism in contrast to heroism for the maintenance of a value to which one is committed.

Adolescence. Puberty initiates a new and turbulent stage of development called adolescence. It begins with efforts to make closer contact with the oposite sex according to the sex-related roles that were developed in pre-adolescence. Masculinity retains a heroic image. It adds to this image a deep interest, sometimes to the point of preoccupation, in the opposite sex. In the early part of this stage, how he makes out with the opposite sex determines in part his status and prestige in the pre-adolescent group. The new interest in the opposite sex, however, very shortly makes the continued functioning of the pre-adolescent group impossible. His comrades in arms in pre-adolescence become his competitors for status with feminine society. Throughout adolescence there continues to be a pleasure in boasting to one's fellows of his conquests in love in much the same fashion as he had boasted of the ships he had robbed as a pirate in pre-adolescence.

For the first time he becomes a rebel against the standards of adult society. In pre-adolescence he had merely developed another set of standards limited in application to his peers. In adolescence he moves in concert with the peer society, which includes males and females, to alter the adult society. He is concerned about the standards of relationships between the sexes, the standards for governing home and family life, the economic and political order. Indeed, he is concerned with reviewing and modifying the entire order. The judgments of peers are of greater importance than those of authorities, especially those which concern about dress, manners and social life. The standards of the last generation are dismissed as "old fogey." It is the adolescent group that *really* knows how one should dress and whether one should go steady or not.

The social contacts with the opposite sex during adolescence involve for the first time treatment of the opposite sex as a person. There is an increasing recognition of the complementary roles played by the two sexes. With the maturing of his masculinity the adolescent is ready to show his ability to provide for and protect a family, but he may lack job-skills. With the maturing of her femininity she is ready to accept his providing for her in order to be able to have and nourish offspring. His pleasure in being seen with a beautiful girl is matched by hers in being treated as beautiful and in being seen with a strong, handsome man. He admires and does not compete with her sociability; she admires and does not compete with his knowledge of the harsher realities of social and economic life. The pattern differs in detail with each "him" and "her"; the discovery of complementary features in their emotional lives must remain the same in order to permit mutuality. When he and she can find fulfillment at the same time within their relationship, mutuality is possible. During the stage of cooperation and sharing, he aims at fulfillment of himself and acquiesces to a give-and-take relationship in order to accomplish his aim. Many times, in cooperating, his own satisfaction comes first: "You scratch my back and then I scratch yours." This mode of interaction with others continues into late adolescence, but the experiences of adolescence make the mutuality of adulthood possible.

Adulthood. Behavioral adulthood is the harvest and fulfillment of all previous experience. It brings harmony and balance and perspective, which are lacking in previous developmental stages. It brings an order and peace not found in previous periods. Identity and commitment to goals is stable and assured. There is the emergence of the capacity to give and to nurture. Until the adult stage, giving is a means of manipulation of others and of self-flattery. In adulthood, giving is the exercise of a capability and therefore fulfillment. With the achievement of maturity and harmony, there emerges the readiness to use these capacities for the benefit of others.

The aim in relationships with the opposite sex is no longer conquest, but mutuality, which includes respect for and participation with the opposite sex in the fulfillment of the deepest and most basic capabilities of each other. The adult is not content merely to have satisfied himself but requires that he has in satisfying himself contributed to the fufillment of the person with whom he interacts.

He is capable of deep loyalty to peers as during pre-adolescence, but a loyalty that is harmonized with his total responsibility. He is not humiliated by the exercise of authority over him nor does he seek to use his authority to humiliate. There is a recognition of the contribution of reasonable authority to the orderly pursuit of social goals. All judgments of him, both from peers and superiors, are given consideration, but in terms of his own standards and values. His effectiveness and competence can no longer be destroyed by unfavorable evaluation of him by either superiors or peers. Above all he must account to himself.

Beyond adulthood. Relatively little is known about the changes in emotional life that occur after the level of adulthood is reached. Theoretically it is possible that progressive and orderly changes in emotional life occur after maturity. Perhaps parenthood introduces changes in the emotional life that are worthy of description. Perhaps the progressive decline in capacity for achievement or sexual activity introduces changes in the emotional life of an adult of a magnitude to warrant consideration of another stage.

The author prefers to think of the developmental scale as extending from birth to death, but it is possible that the changes in emotional life beyond adulthood are only of the magnitude of phases and do not reflect major reorientations. The term development is often understood as a progressive increase in size or value; the author uses the word to mean a progressive and gradual unfolding. Thus, whether emotional life beyond adulthood represents an increase or decrease, it might still be described as part of a developmental process.

The developmental process and interpersonal relationships

The developmental process contains, and is thus defined by, a series of altered patterns of interpersonal relationships. The pattern of action and experience at any point on the developmental scale determines whether emotional life moves forward, backward or remains static. Normality is change; deviation is reinforcement of the current pattern. Development is a successive, constantly improving approximation of adult maturity. Movement is steady and continuous within stages, but uneven and discontinuous between stages. Major changes in goals occur between stages, and each stage has its own special problems. What is rewarding in interaction with others changes from stage to stage.

Each pattern of interpersonal relationships may be regarded as preparatory to the next later point of the developmental scale. The intense relationship to the mother in infancy is preparatory to the extension and elaboration of this kind of relationship with a host of authorities in childhood, which modifies the pattern. The increasing emotional significance of peers during childhood is preparatory to the development of a social organization of peers in pre-adolescence. The development of ways to maintain self-respect with the family is preparatory to the elaboration and refinement of these operations with the host of authorities in childhood and with peers in pre-adolescence.

Each point of the developmental scale provides fulfillment for the one preceding it. Fulfillment means the exercise of a capability, a pattern of interpersonal relationships, which results in increased capacity, a better and socially more effective pattern of relationships. It is progressive growth to maturity. The interest in peers stimulated by the mother during late infancy finds fulfillment in childhood. The increased significance of peers and the independence of these relationships from the mother achieved during childhood find fulfillment in the development of a complex pattern of relationships to peers during pre-adolescence, which includes in-group and out-group forms.

Growth tends to be cumulative, with much retained from all earlier developmental levels. The patterns of behavior in relating to peers of the same sex that emerge during pre-adolescence are retained in the adult stage. There is still a satisfaction in a "night out with the boys." There may be participation in a club that permits only men or only women. Many of the behavioral patterns of each stage may be carried over into the next later stage with little or no modification. The behavioral pattern has reached a more or less permanent form at that stage. It may be used in pursuit of the new goals of the next stage. On the other hand, many of the behavioral patterns at any particular stage are in transitional form. The patterns of masculine behavior, for example, in pre-adolescence are in transitional form. They will undergo modification in adolescence before reaching permanent form in adulthood. Each stage then presents to the next stage behavioral patterns that are in transitional and permanent form.

The kind of preferred interpersonal activity changes from one stage to the next, but all types of interpersonal activities are retained. The dominant interpersonal activity of infancy is receiving, which is retained through all successive stages. The dominant and characteristic activity of late infancy is possession, which continues to give satisfaction in all succeeding stages. The cooperation and sharing of childhood undergoes modification and refinement during pre-adolescence and adolescence, but retains its applicability in adulthood. Giving and mutuality are characteristic of adulthood but receiving, having, cooperating and sharing are retained as alternates. The infant is capable of doing little else except receiving; it is a part of his limitation. The adult may derive satisfaction from many of the modes of interpersonal behavior and he is not compelled by limitation to use either one. Increased maturity is manifested in a larger number of patterns as well as change of preferred pattern.

The basic concepts of interpersonal organization undergo progressive modification of meaning with movement along the developmental scale. At the level of infancy, group has no meaning. In late infancy it is no more than an aggregate of people. In childhood it is something that is brought into existence and managed by an adult. The child's responsibility is to do what the adult directs him to do. If the adult does not come to the meeting, the group does not develop. The children relate themselves to each other in smaller patterns and in activities that are different from those of the group activity. Not before pre-adolescence are groups of peers formed that are relatively independent of adults. These groups are recreational. Groups with serious, social purpose are organized and controlled by adults. In adolescence and adulthood one participates, for the first time, in groups of a serious, social purpose that are not controlled and managed by an adult. The concept of the leader undergoes modification corresponding to that of the group. The leader is at first definitely a superior and has full responsibility for the functioning of the group. If he does not come one day, he is responsible for nothing being accomplished. What a leader is like, then, changes in accordance with the purpose of the group; if it is serious, the leader is a superior; if it is recreational, he may be a peer. This is elaborated and refined until the leader becomes one chosen by the group to fulfill a purpose or function designated by the group. The specific behavior that gives fulfillment and increases self-respect progressively changes with developmental level.

Discussion and references

The author's viewpoint throughout this book is first, last and always that of therapist. The reasons for including a description of the normal developmental process in a book completely and singlemindedly devoted to therapy are several. The changing characteristics of behavioral organization during normal growth define an invariant sequence which establishes for therapy a hierarchy of goals leading to adult maturity. The invariant sequence also serves as a yardstick for measuring therapeutic accomplishment. It establishes clear, objective, behavioral criteria for the evaluation of the effectiveness of a therapeutic program. The sequence discloses the direction of development, and with only a minimum of imagination one can discover ways to facilitate and support this normal progression to the next higher level. Normal development is a rich source of material for developing the methods and techniques of an effective therapy. This fertile field has been largely neglected in the preoccupation of therapists with psychopathology. The author's system of using normal growth as the model for therapeutic intervention is in sharp contrast to those systems aimed primarily at the remedy of psychopathology, such as the psychoanalytic system (Fenichel, 1945).

As Rosen (1964) has positively and pointedly acclaimed, the confusion of viewpoints of therapist and scientist can only result in poor therapy and unnecessary suffering of the client. The objective of the therapist is to remedy, to bring relief, which is a more limited and focused aim than the scientific objective of full and complete understanding. In making his theoretical decisions, the author was guided by the objectives of the therapist, not those of the scientist. This does not mean that he opposes the objective of science nor that he thinks his objective is morally or socially superior. It means that he does not believe that the viewpoint of the scientist—neutral, aloof, committed only to knowing, not influencing—is suitable for the therapist, who must use scientific information to develop a systematic approach to changing behavior. On the other hand, careful and scientific development of the viewpoint of therapist can only contribute to, not detract from, the fulfillment of the goal of science.

The author's major sources for methodological considerations are books edited by Helson (1951) and Marx (1951). The article by Preston (1951) is an excellent summary of major methodological issues. The guiding consideration in making methodological choices was to make decisions that would give homogeneous constructs for conceptualization of the normal developmental process, the developmental deviations and the therapeutic process. In addition, the author's aim was to develop constructs at a low level of inference that were as clearly and closely related as possible to what the therapist could see as an observer of the therapeutic process. The focus of the author's theory (Brunswik, 1951) is overt behavioral acts viewed in the context of the interpersonal relationship of which they are a part. The theory is molar, deductive, objective and operational. It does not use intervening variables (Tolman, 1951) and rejects reductionism.

In regard to the subject matter of this chapter, the formal properties of the construct stage proposed by the author for the development of emotional life are the same as those proposed by Piaget (Flavell, 1963). These properties are: 1) constant sequence, 2) integration of earlier structures into later ones, 3) the parts fit together to make a larger whole, and 4) initial preparation culminates in final achievement (Flavell, 1963, pp. 19-21). Piaget's work demostrates that cognition develops according to such stages, but perception does not. Erikson (1963) proposes very similar if not identical properties for the stages of child development. Sullivan (1953) describes stages of development with many references to what can go wrong in each stage. The descriptions of Sullivan and Erikson are from an intrapsychic point of view but those of Piaget from an observers' point of view which is also the author's viewpoint. Sullivan's stages extend only through adolescence; he does not describe the emotional life of the adult. On the matter of stages beyond adulthood, Benedek (1959) proposes that parenthood results in significant changes in emotional life.

Loevinger (1966) in a valuable article presents the implications of theoretical models of growth for the measurement of ego development. In particular, the article makes clear that it is necessary to know whether a behavioral attribute is a polar variable (continuous) or a milestone sequence (curvilinear). The article clarifies many of the methodological problems of actually measuring therapeutic gain—the author's criterion. The emphasis in the author's description that is given to interaction with associates outside the family, especially associates that can participate at the same developmental level (peers) in playful activity, finds experimental documentation in the studies of Piaget (Flavell, 1963, pp. 156-157) and Harlow and Harlow (1962). Men and monkeys play their way to adult maturity.

The author's major source of observations for the description

of the developmental scale was growth during a therapeutic process, not normal growth of children. The close correspondence of
conclusions reached through observation of the therapeutic process with those reached by Piaget through observation of children
at different developmental levels strongly supports the validity of
the conclusions and the equation of growth and therapeutic gain.
For those interested in studying growth, the therapeutic process
offers the major advantage of a reduced time span which makes
vertical studies more feasible than they are of normal growth.

The author believes that the invariant sequence of the developmental process is culture-free, a conclusion that has been supported by several studies of conceptual development (Tuddenham,
1966). A stage may not develop in a culture, but its place in the
sequence is everywhere the same. Thus, some cultures may not
provide adequate conditions to support growth all the way to
maturity. The author is opposed to culturally relative norms. A
foot that is bound in any culture is not a normal foot. Why should
the growth of an adult individual that is short of adult maturity
be considered normal merely because the agency of the blocking
of growth is a society rather than a few individuals? The author
joins Burrow (Gault, 1953) to the extent of accepting the idea
that societies as well as a few individuals can block the natural
process of growth to adult maturity.

The author is clearly on the side of Jahoda (1958) in her
affirmation that mental health is more than the mere absence of
mental illness. Mental health is the manifestation of the pattern
of interpersonal relationships appropriate to one's physical development and length of opportunity for experience. Because rate
of development varies from person to person, fine discriminations
for the degree of mental health cannot be made. On the other
hand, it is valid to conclude that a twelve-year-old child whose
emotional life is that of late infancy is low in mental health. In
such a case there will be symptoms and psychopathology, but these
findings do not define the basic problem. It is the absence of
positive growth that is the essence of the poor mental health.
Efforts to improve mental health should be directed toward stimulating this growth, not toward the mere removal of symptoms.

Focused and limited intervention, which is not covered in this book, when required by consideration of the little time available for treatment, should be directed toward behavior patterns that block growth, toward starting the flow of growth, not merely toward the reduction of anxiety and depression.

Deviations of the Developmental Process

At this point in history the odds are very great against an actual developmental sequence following the course outlined in the previous chapter. The educators of the children themselves have histories of an imperfect developmental process. The lack of maturity of the educators means that they prefer and tend to insist upon a pattern of relationship with those they teach that is below the adult level. Even when the educator has an adult emotional life, there is still sickness and death and economic disaster and cultural dislocation and a host of other things to disrupt the continuity and stability of the nurturing interpersonal relationship. In our day the supervision of the developmental process is still largely entrusted to the mythical and magical maternal instinct. People experience failure and loss of self-respect in applying for professional help to overcome the inadequacies of their developmental history. All of these conditions mean that very few people reach the level of adulthood. A great many of those who do reach maturity are easily disrupted in this mode of functioning and return to earlier and experientially safer levels of functioning.

The author's view that deviation is the rule rather than the exception leads him to reject the statistical definition and to accept as the standard an idealized scale which is presented in the previous chapter on developmental process. Each level of physiological development, which may be roughly delimited by reference to age, should be associated with a certain level of emotional life. A developmental deviation is revealed by a discrepancy between the expected and the actual level of emotional life. A definition in these terms is useful in categorizing the extent or degree of a developmental deviation but offers little guidance for its treatment or correction. For the latter purpose an understanding of the basic interpersonal pattern associated with the production of the deviation is more useful. This chapter is primarily concerned with the basic interpersonal pattern which results in the psychotic deviation. By way of contrast and in order to more clearly define the psychotic deviation, the basic patterns of the neurotic and character disorder deviation are also presented.

It should be emphasized that the author considers the characteristic interpersonal history of the individual essential to the identification of the psychotic deviation. The concept overlaps but is not identical with schizophrenia, which is defined symptomatically, not developmentally. All instances of psychotic deviation probably lie within the category of schizophrenia, but the reverse is not true. There are corresponding considerations of the neurotic deviation. Many of the conditions now labeled psychoneurotic are produced by the pattern of mother-child relationship described below. On the other hand, some conditions so described are *not,* as for example, the anxiety state associated with a real loss of security, as from loss of employment, physical illness, and marital conflict. The point is that the author limits the applicability of these concepts to the developmental histories as described. The concepts have etiological implications by definition.

All developmental deviations tend to be self-perpetuating. The interpersonal pattern which produces the deviation trains the person to prefer a certain pattern of relationships to other people. He chooses people who will participate in this pattern with him, people who will "play his game." He rejects as associates people who do not treat him and regard him as he expects and who are disappointed or angry at the way he acts toward them. By his choice of associates he introduces systematic biases into his experience. He bases his ideas of what he is like, what other people are like, what they expect of him, and what he can expect of them on his experiences with these selected associates. His experiences with people therefore continually confirm his beliefs because he has eliminated contradictory evidence in his choice of associates. It is the breaking up of this self-perpetuating pattern and the broadening of the individual's experience that constitutes the work of therapy. The author rejects the theory that the sole basis

for the continuity of a developmental deviation is historical or
intrapsychic; the current interpersonal experience of the person
tends to perpetuate the deviation.

The most fundamental basis for classifying a developmental
deviation is the quality of the nurturing interpersonal relationship in which it is generated. The nurturing interpersonal relationship of the psychotic and neurotic deviations are blocking and
constricting ones, respectively. The character disorder derives
from a conflict so intense that its emotions completely dominate
every other consideration and govern behavior. The second most
important consideration is the way the person attempts to cope
with the problem presented to him in the nurturing interpersonal
relationship. In the psychotic deviation, for example, a basic distinction can be made between a response that undertakes adaptation to the nurturing interpersonal relationship and one which
attempts to avoid or escape the problem. The attempt to adapt
produces manifest behavior of an infantile quality. The avoidance
reaction produces an unresponsiveness to other people or a responsiveness that is formal or in some other way stylized, as by an
occupational role. The person may be able to respond to others
in the role of doctor, lawyer or soldier, but not as an individual
person. The playing of such stylized roles prevents activation of
the immature patterns of behavior; it avoids the pattern of being
an infant in the care of a towering giant. The differences which
result from the manner in which the mother blocks the child's
relationships to other people, which is described below, provides
another example of different elaborations of the same basic
problem.

A third, but most subordinate classification of developmental
deviations refers to the current status of the relationship between
the preferred and actual interpersonal pattern. Disturbed, agitated,
hyperactive, frantic behavior results from a wide discrepancy;
stable, orderly, settled behavior results from a correspondence.
The behavioral problem presented by a client may thus be described briefly in terms of the basic nature of the interpersonal
problem, the elaboration of this problem in the history of the
client and the present correspondence between the interpersonal
pattern he has learned and his current social life.

The manifest behavior of a client may be understood in terms of these three perspectives, each one of which provides additional understanding. Let us suppose that a client takes little note of his surroundings. If he is spoken to, he seldom makes any reply or even gives any signal indicating that he knows he is being spoken to. The view from the most subordinate level raises the question of whether this behavior is maintained day after day or whether it is subject to sudden shifts from very withdrawn to very socially aggressive. If it becomes unsettled, then a search would be made for recent and current disillusionment. The client has probably been confronted with information that destroys his hope that a current relationship will provide the infantile satisfactions that he expects. If he has used the avoidance pattern of elaboration, a relationship that threatens to become personal rather than formal may precipitate a crisis, which is expressed in the unstable behavior. On the other hand, if the withdrawn orientation is maintained day after day, it probably represents his preferred pattern of relating himself to people. It is an expression of himself, as contrasted to a reaction to a current crisis. The perspective from the level of elaboration distinguishes between withdrawn behavior that originates from a lack of stimulation and encouragement to relate himself to others and withdrawn behavior due to the avoidance of relationships. The two may be readily distinguished by more careful observation and description of the client's behavior. The first may be best described as apathy; it is an uncomplicated, unemotional lack of interest in other people. He pays very little attention to people because he has no interest in them. On the other hand, a withdrawal based on avoidance is associated with taking a great deal of notice of people, watching them carefully in order to protect one's self from their treachery. The withdrawn behavior is watchful waiting, in readiness to either fight or flee. Viewed from the most fundamental level, the withdrawn behavior means that relationships to other people are blocked, as contrasted to merely being limited to those in which the client is expected to be quiet and unobtrusive. The distinction notes whether he has been trained not to relate to other people or whether he has been trained to relate to them in this particular way. All of these distinctions have direct and near self-evident implications for the correction of the developmental deviation in therapy.

The psychotic deviation

By far the most profound and destructive developmental deviations are associated with the failure of the mother to use her absolutely dominant emotional significance to establish and nurture the child's relationships with other children and adults. Instead she uses her power to destroy any interest in or significant interactions with any person other than herself. The course of development associated with this mother-child relationship is called psychotic deviation.

The following excerpts from a single therapy session with a man in his fifties illustrate the principle of the mother blocking relationships with people. (C. = client; T. = therapist).

C.   Kind of peculiar people in my opinion.

T.   Your grandmother?

C.   The whole outfit. My mother's side of the family. Very peculiar to me.

T.   How were they peculiar?

C.   They kind of set themselves on a pedestal as I can remember it, to a certain extent. Always wanted you to associate with one element of people. My thinking has always been you can't do that, it's not that easy. In other words a person that hasn't got the economical background and other background, they are kind of particular, too, about who they associated with. You've got to associate with who you can find, has always been my opinion.
Nobody ever seemed to be good enough that I went with. People had more money than I did and better positions than I did; they had their opinions on those things, too. It's not that easy. A person without to associate with people that have. They do a little eliminating themselves as to who they associate with.

T. Your grandmother wanted you to associate with the best people?

C. My mother was more so than my grandmother, but I don't remember too much about it. Probably I should, but I don't. It's been so many years ago. It wasn't that easy. It wasn't that simple. The best people, as I said before, are particular who they associate with and a person who doesn't have position and background can't associate with the better element of people, it just don't work that way.

T. The people your mother wanted you to associate with didn't want to accept you?

C. That's it. I did work different jobs when I was little to get some money and with some people it was kind of degrading because I had to make money and I sell newspapers. That's the only way I could get money. I just didn't have it handed to me on a silver platter like some people. The world as I see it is awfully full of discrimination, partiality and injustice and hypocrisy . . .

C. My mother told me many times that I should have left the town because my father was what he was and who he was and how people felt about him and I never could get anywhere because of it. I hate to harp on these things, but . . .

C. When I was in the hospital here before, I had what I considered compliments from various factions in the hospital. I told her [his mother] that one time. I didn't tell her what they told me. She said, "Well, they only told you that to make you feel good." So she just can't get away from the way she's tried to destroy me, at least that's my conception of it. I just don't believe the doctors in this hospital would have said the things to me if they hadn't have felt it. I might be wrong, but I don't think so . . .

C. There's never been any closeness in my family.

C. She [his mother] said he [social worker] said I had a mighty sad life. I was talking to my oldest sister one time about it

and she said, "I wonder if she told him the truth." There
is a lot of behind the scene, underhanded action going on.

T.   In your family?

C.   Yes. I know one time when I was about 15 years old, 15 or
17, I rode a bicycle out to my father's mother's place. That's
about 15 miles out from the town and she said, "What are
you city slickers coming into the country for?" So that country people have that feeling about me as being physically
inferior. Mother said because of my father the people in
town would have that viewpoint, too. You can't win for losing in my situation . . .

C.   Like when I married my wife. Before we got married, I was
talking to her father about it and he asked me what my
father did. I told him he was a farmer. He said, "Just a hill-
billy farmer, huh!" Some people don't seem to realize what
—how that those remarks can force a person into various
reaction and various opinions and beliefs.

T.   What have they made you believe?

C.   Well, it's destroyed my faith in the human race.

The way in which the mother blocks the child from relating
himself to other people shows many variations which change the
details of the consequences. The mother may be indifferent to
the child and out of her indifference simply fail to take enough
interest to introduce the child to others and direct his first fledg-
ling attempts to interact with them. She cares for the physical
needs of the child but shows little interest or pleasure or dis-
pleasure in him, nor does she play with the child. With no stimulation or active engagement with any person, the child is himself
indifferent and apathetic. The continuation of this patterning of
interpersonal events through infancy leaves the child unable to
establish relationships with classmates and teachers when he enters
school. He appears to have only a vague awareness of either himself or other people and practically no ideas about how to relate
himself to people. His few experiences with people provide him
such little information of what they are like that he is free to draw

almost any kind of conclusion about them. His experiences are too limited to contradict any conclusion. Life is endless nothingness. He has never been stimulated to do things, to accept challenges, to commit himself to an assignment. No one cares if he does anything or not. Seemingly, no one cares whether he lives or dies. His experiences leave him with a more profound and complete feeling of helplessness than most people who have not been subjected to such indifference from birth onward can imagine. His deep apathy and hopelessness, generated during infancy, result in a perpetuation of the deficiencies of his interpersonal experience in childhood and adolescence. He is a drag socially. He is easily ignored. He is almost eerily unobtrusive. No one takes notice of him. If anyone should initiate an interaction with him, he is so unresponsive and gives so little feedback of any interest in continuing the exchange that he is quickly dropped.

If the maternal indifference is combined with deep, quiet, icy contempt, it results in a slight increase in the active disturbance of the child. The contempt of the mother toward him becomes a part of himself. His showing of contempt toward himself elevates his level of activity slightly. He may even undertake a subtle and quiet battle with the mother in defense of his honor. If so, it is a one-sided and losing battle from the beginning. Nevertheless, it does tend to soften the intensity of the apathy and helplessness. There is a fight, a little one, but a fight.

When the mother is indifferent, there is a possibility that someone else will take an interest in the child and help him learn to establish an interpersonal relationship. Someone else may provide the stimulation that the indifferent mother cannot give. With the possessive mother such hope is doomed. She not only fails to introduce the child to other people but actively and jealously opposes any chance significance that other people may have for him. Her opposition is presented in her actions toward the child as being based on the noblest of human motives; a mother's love for her offspring. If the child speaks affectionately of a neighbor, the mother is very shortly warning of people who deceive and trick to victimize other people. She warns that the neighbor is using the child for his own purposes. She becomes cold and distant and deeply angry at any mention of the neighbor. Her action communicates "choose between that malicious, lying, tricking, deceiving neighbor and your lovely, kind, sweet, devoted, self-sacrificing mother." If the child takes an interest in playing with other children, he very soon learns from the mother that these playmates are not good enough for him. He is warned that they will corrupt him, get him into trouble and abandon him. In this way the possessive mother destroys the child's opportunities of building relationships with other people. She thus makes him helplessly and hopelessly dependent upon her. She presents to the child a picture of other people as being deceitful, vicious, self-seeking and treacherous. She creates a perceptual bias of expecting these kinds of actions from other people. The child has too few experiences with people to arrive at his own conclusion. Even those experiences which he does have are highly colored by his expectation of treachery. He is lonely. He is in a hostile world alone with his mother. He must be constantly on his guard in order to survive. His distrust of other people naturally causes offense to them. Because of his attitude he has more and more experiences of being rejected, of being the object of anger, of being the object of retaliation. These inevitable experiences, given his attitude, serve to confirm and perpetuate his approach to other people which continues his interpersonal difficulties. In response to the impact of these experiences with people, he develops elaborate ways of protecting himself against the treachery of people. This defending of himself tends to soften the intensity of the feelings of helplessness and apathy. However, the odds are overwhelmingly against him, which generates feelings of inadequacy and helplessness.

Since all of his meager satisfactions must come from the mother, the intensity of his needs in this relationship is elevated to such a high level that it inevitably must result in frustration. Separation from the mother, for example, is an extremely disturbing experience. It destroys his only security. Frequently he develops a pattern of intense, but subdued rage upon separation. He may commit destructive, intensely hostile acts in his violent reaction to being left and rejected. The satisfactions that children, in general, are gaining in relationships with the mother *and* other members of the family *and* neighbors *and* other children, the child of the possessive mother must gain from her. It is impossible for her to give all of these satisfactions. The child must inevitably be frustrated, which threatens the mother. It is intolerable to her that she should be a disappointment to her child. She forces him to hide his disillusionment from her. Yet her awareness of the child's unhappiness is fuel for her contempt.

The experiences of the child with either the indifferent or the possessive mother leave the child with only a vague notion of what he is like, and even this is limited to the one perspective acquired in the relationship to the mother. He has no opportunity to experience evaluations of himself with neighbors, family, children, teachers and so on. His pattern of interpersonal relationships remains at the level of infancy as he becomes physically an adult. Even worse, there is added either apathy or distrust of other people, which causes offense and brings rejection. There are no satisfying, pleasant relationships with people. All of his experiences are frustrating, tense, degrading. Naturally he learns to spend a great deal of his time alone. Even when he is away from people physically, he carries with him his degradation of being unacceptable to other people. He feels unloved, unloveable. He is miserable, but the persistence of such noxious experiences tends to dull the pain. There is adaptation to psychological distress as there is to physical pain.

Apparently a person whose emotional life remains at the infantile level can go through childhood without producing a social crisis. Usually, at least, his behavior does not become so disturbing to agents of the community as to produce an insistence upon his removal. It is obvious, however, that the emotional life of such a person is poorly suited to manage the impact of puberty and the push it gives toward close contacts with another person. Sexuality remains at an infantile level. Sexual feeling is spread over the entire body and is not focused on the genital area. The deprivation of experiences with people has left a lack of skill in making himself understood and in being understood. He is clumsy and awkward in social contacts. His concept of himself is too poorly developed for him to judge the impact he is having on another person. He has too little and too biased a concept of other people to interpret what they mean when they interact with him. What skill he does have in dealing with people is largely limited to authority-subordinate relationships. He is especially poorly equipped to manage a peer relationship and most especially one in which there are sexual implications. Under the impact of social change associated with puberty, even the limited degree of order and stability that he has been able to achieve may break down into a state of confusion, perplexity and desperate excitement, into a behavioral collapse. The more intense and the more stable are the attitudes of apathy and helplessness, the less likely is a behavioral collapse. The indifference carries him through without a collapse, but he is totally unprepared for anything other than being someone's baby. If someone takes care of his physical needs, provides food and shelter for him, he may remain in the community. Usually he gets into trouble only because he fails to provide for himself, not because he threatens anybody. He seems to have no recognition or feeling for the need to support and maintain himself. It is as if he continued to expect the mother to care for him as if he were an infant. The child of the possessive mother may escape behavioral collapse during puberty if he has achieved some order and stability in defending himself against the treachery of others.

Both the indifferent and the distrustful individual arrive at puberty and then physical adulthood with an emotional life like that of an infant, with some destructive additions. Their only pattern of interpersonal relationship is that of an infant to the mother. Their increasing physical maturity and their exposure to the world of people results in other people trying to establish relationships with them according to patterns that are not in their behavioral repertoire and in which they cannot participate. They are expected to do and be things that they are not and do not. They may develop skill at pretense or it may be clear that they are confused and bewildered by such expectations.

The deprivation of maturing experiences is vast for both the indifferent and suspicious individual. They never have all of the experiences with peers and the host of authorities associated with school life that provde a basis for evaluation of one's self in the perspective of the community. They do not have the experiences that provide a basis for appreciation of the differences among people. They do not have the experiences that teach how a man or woman is supposed to behave. They lack the experience to create for themselves an interpretation of their masculine or feminine identity that is suitable to them and to society. Only a progressively broadening system of interpersonal relationships could provide them the experiences necessary for moving toward maturity. Such a broadening pattern of interpersonal relationships could not occur without active support and certainly not against active opposition of the mother.

The neurotic deviation

The neurotic deviation results from a highly qualified acceptance of the child by the mother. The child is acceptable only if he demonstrates or seems to demonstrate certain qualities decided on by the mother without regard to him. The content of the qualities is unimportant. It might be cleanliness, kindness, docility or beauty. What is significant is that the actions of the mother toward the child convey acceptance if he seems to fit into her categories and convey rejection if he does not. She gives him the feeling that he exists for her only if he fits her categories. It is so important to the mother for the child to have these characteristics that she insists upon them before the child is ready to become interested in them himself or to appreciate their realistic merit. Because of the actions of the mother toward him, he comes to experience, independent of his direct interaction with her, the feeling of being worthy if he demonstrates these qualities and a feeling of being utterly worthless if he fails to demonstrate them.

A history of this kind of interaction with the mother inevitably results in a constriction of experience; it inevitably requires the avoidance of some situations in order to insure that one always shows the specified qualities. To be always clean, for example, requires that one avoid many situations that could, if one participated in them, provide useful information about oneself and other people. The urgency of demonstrating the specified qualities at all times inevitably leads to falsification. The constriction placed upon the child by the mother is naturally resented and therefore opposed, but subtly so. He can have dirty underwear and a dirty ear on the side out of the mother's view at the table.

He falsifies himself as absolutely clean. He knows it is not true. He is apprehensive lest his deceit be discovered, his hypocrisy, and he be rejected and abandoned. His anxiety upon being confronted by any information that would demonstrate or emphasize his duplicity and his failure to stay within the bounds of the specified qualities encourages him to overlook these aspects of the outside world. He tends to lose contact with what kind of person he is and to retain information only about what kind of person he should be. Yet there can be no gap between what he is and what he should be without devastating emotional consequences for him. The variety of his relationships with people is constricted by the absolute necessity for maintaining these qualities. He demands that anyone to whom he relates himself must recognize that he possesses these qualities. If anyone questions or conveys disbelief, he is immediately disliked and dropped. Since there is usually ample grounds for disbelief, he separates himself from people who call a spade a spade. He forms relationships with people who will play his game of hypocrisy with him. This bias in his choice of relationship distorts his experience and aids him in developing patterns of behavior which avoid confrontation with valid information about himself. Even so, reality is persistent. He must become skillful in distorting his interpretations of incoming information in order to maintain his false concept of himself.

His security is threatened by any information, either from interpersonal events or from his own inner feelings that contradict his false concept of himself. The maintenance of this concept requires a great deal of effort and it is always risky, for he can never tell when someone is going to slip up on him and confront him with his hypocrisy. He develops a strong preference for relationships that are perfectly predictable, that have no surprises. But such predictable behavior is itself a serious deviation, and the people he associates with will, therefore, supply distorted information. His relationships are limited to those that do not correct his deviation but rather reinforce it.

Because of the problem of maintaining his false concept, his relationships with people expose him to strain and tension. They are burdensome for him. Nevertheless, the mother permits relationships with others. She may even insist upon them. The mother in this pattern tends to use the child for her own aggrandizement. She insists that the child be clean in order to boast to all of the neighbors about how early he was toilet trained and how neat he is. She insists that the child be beautiful in order to reap the dubious honor for herself. She insists that the child be good to permit her boast of what an outstanding, magnificent, adorable, heaven-sent mother she is and how unfortunate it is that other mothers do not learn from her example. Her security thus comes to depend upon the child always demonstrating the qualities that she specifies. His failure to do so makes her insecure and inadequate. He is acceptable to her only if he is the kind of child she demands.

The constriction of his relationships to other people heightens his dependency on the mother. She usually has a reduced capacity for satisfying dependency needs. She has a reduced ability to receive and respond to his appeals for care and affection. Often these appeals are at odds with the qualities that she demands. Hence, the child must bury even from his sight his own dependency. The people with whom the child chooses to form a relationship usually have the same impaired potential for expressions of affection that the mother does. They are too much like robots to communicate warmth and affection. Even their verbalized affection takes on a cold formal tone. Spontaneity is too unpredictable to be tolerated except under heavy guard, which destroys it. The high level of his dependency, as in the psychotic deviation, greatly elevates the probability of frustration, disappointment and disillusionment. For example, it elevates the psychological trauma of separation from the mother. In the ideal developmental sequence, the child moves from the secure relationship with the mother to satisfying and secure relationships with many other people. His dependency on the mother is overcome not by some act of will on his part, but by a gradual development of other relationships, which are supported and nurtured by her. He moves from security to security; not from security to the unknown. In the neurotic deviation, the child's strong dependency elevates the significance of the evaluations of the mother. It makes the continuation of her highly conditional love all the more imperative; it is absolutely essential to his positive self regard. In order to maintain her love, he must preserve the static and false concept. Thus because of his strong dependency, the maintenance of the false concept becomes imperative.

The results of the desperate necessity to maintain the false concept are many and far-reaching. It provides a point of departure for discussion of the inadequacies of the interpersonal relationships of a person who shows this kind of developmental deviation. There is a reduced probability of satisfaction in relationships with people. The child is not free to express his emotional life; his action tends to prevent fulfillment. His emotional life may be at a level of requests for guidance and reassurance that his actions and decisions are good ones. His actions may be highly independent, self-assured and he may even scorn and devaluate the significance of others' opinions of his actions. He therefore acts in a way to reduce to nil the probability of his getting the kinds of responses from other people that his fulfillment and development require. Thus he insures his own frustration. His false self-concept, as he presents it in interactions with other people, will tend to attract people to him who want and expect him to act in accord with this false concept. Thus if he is acting in a highly independent manner when in fact he would like to be dependent, he attracts people who are dependent and who would like a relationship with a highly independent person. He therefore establishes relationships with people whose security would be threatened by expressions deriving from his real level of maturity. Such actions would be a betrayal of the bargain he made in the formation of these relationships. In the relationships he has chosen, self-fulfilling actions are associated with failure in his obligations and therefore a loss of positive regard from his associates. If they should occur, such actions are met with a cold, rejecting response. His interactions with people continually confirm his belief that rejection and ruin are in store for him if he should fail to live up to the false concept. In the ideal development, the individual is free to act in accord with the situation, the preferences of himself and those of his associates; he is thus free to develop patterns for many different kinds of relationships. He is free to be an observer, a participator, a leader, an objector, a rebel, a spy and so on. From the diversity of his relationships, he develops a highly differentiated concept of himself with a diversity of behavioral patterns. He can be many things. He can form and maintain relationships of highly diverse quality. He is not compelled from fear and actual experience of rejection if he deviates from a highly circumscribed type of relationship. In contrast, in the neurotic deviation, the individual may form relationships with many different people, but since he constricts his relationships to people who will play his game with him, he does not learn many different patterns of interpersonal relationship; he tends to re-enact and strengthen the pattern of his relationship with the mother by the way he interacts with all of the different people.

The character disorder deviation

The essence of the character disorder deviation appears to be open rejection, even more or less public rejection, of the child by one or more major contributors to his education, frequently the father but sometimes the mother. The critical difference between this pattern and that of the indifferent or possessive mother is that the parental figure does not insist that he loves the child, that his every action is in behalf of the child, that the child is ungrateful for thinking that the parent is hostile or that the parent is a personification of righteousness. The assumption of moral superiority by the indifferent and the possessive mother forces the resistance and fight of the child underground and associates it with guilt. Open hostility of the parent permits an undisguised, direct fight from the child. Parent and child make it clear to each other and without apology that they do not like one another. Nothing the child does or says or is pleases the parent and he is direct in saying so. The child becomes just as direct in his communication of dislike for the parent.

The consequences for the emotional life of the child of this pattern are more diverse than those of the psychotic pattern. Perhaps this results from the fact that the child is freer to form relationships that have a function of substitute parents. One common result is a lack of any ability to feel or sympathize or show any consideration for the other person. At the same time, he may develop an extremely high skill in seeming to understand and share the other person's feelings. But if such interaction is observed over a matter of weeks or a few months it turns out that "seeming to understand the other person" was part of a well-staged act to use the other person for his own superficial satisfaction. His action elicits admiration or guilt or hope of gain or fear of exposure, which he then uses to seduce or coerce with no more regard for the person than he would have for a thing that gave him satisfaction.

Frequently his open battle with the parental figure is also a destruction of any positive regard or acceptance of personal obligation for the standards of society. In normal development the rules of society become a part of the individual out of his positive regard for his parents. The absence of any such positive regard for the rejecting parent leaves the rules outside of the individual, and he may even actively oppose and challenge the rules in the same way he fought with the parental figure. His lack of respect for the parents is transferred directly and fully to his attitude toward society; his open battle against them becomes an open battle against society.

Often the battle with the parent seems to have the objective of forcing him to give or robbing him of satisfactions. Many of his later actions in his relationships with people and with society have a similar quality. It is as if he felt he had been cheated and was intent upon gaining restitution. The compensation he demands and takes is infantile satisfaction. His gain from taking advantage of and using other people is often of little monetary value and seldom does it contribute toward any improvement of himself or his position in society. He appears to gain his satisfaction from cheating, making fools and degrading other people, not from the objects themselves that are attained in this way. His objective appears to be the degradation of people, not the material gain or the improvement of his opportunities that may be associated with his anti-social behavior.

Continuity of relationships over a period of years is out of the question in this kind of development. Even six months is a long time for him to carry on a relationship. An hour, a few days or several weeks is the more usual length. The relationships are totally artificial and fail to express anything genuine or to provide

any fulfillment. They are well-staged acts which have been per-
formed for many audiences. They are repeat performances. They
are re-enactments of the hostile battle with the openly rejecting
parent.

This kind of development permits no greater differentiation
of self, no better evaluation of self than does the psychotic development. While the individual develops relationships with many
different people, the pattern is the same. No new patterns are
discovered and developed. The incoming information is the same;
his action is the same. His behavior does not change, which is the
essence of deviation. The interaction in these relationships thus
merely serves to confirm, not to change his beliefs and his way
of life. His relationships do not promote his growth. They provide no new concepts of other people or himself, nor do they
elaborate those he has already. A new relationship merely adds
another notch to his belt. His experiences do not permit him to
develop friendships or be a member of a family. He is as alone
and isolated as he would be if he related to no one. Life has only
one goal, one satisfaction for him: the punishment and coercion
and manipulation of the hostile parent.

Discussion and references

The ultimate criterion of a behavioral deviation is developmental
history. This is no different in principle from the learning theory
analysis of behavior in terms of number and scheduling of rein-
forcements, temporal relationship between responses and reinforcement and such. The principle is that knowledge of the
conditions under which manifest behavior developed permits a
degree of prediction and control not otherwise possible.

Establishing a history of developmental deviation determines
that a behavioral deviation is present: 1) which is independent of
other conditions or problems, such as those of a legal, religious,
medical or educational nature, which may also be present, 2) which
is not and cannot be corrected by the alteration of other conditions or problems that may be present, and 3) which requires a
program of intervention specifically designed for its correction.

In the author's view the fundamental nature of all behavioral deviations is immaturity; the only means by which immaturity can be corrected is exposure to an increasingly broader range of experience. The immaturity, which is a pattern of interpersonal relationships below what is expected for level of physical development and length of opportunity for experience, may be directly manifest or it may be blocked from activation by incompatible responses. This division of the immaturity is given further elaboration in the chapter "Achieving Therapeutic Gain" (page 81) in terms of approach and avoidance behavior. The idea of the degree of behavioral stability or disturbance being dependent upon the relationship between preferred and current interpersonal pattern is highly compatible with the theory of cognitive congruence as this is applied by McRenolds (1960) to schizophrenia and by Secord and Backman (1961) to the general problem of behavioral stability.

The mention of immaturity as a significant feature of psychopathology or behavioral deviation is characteristic of the literature. Rosen (1964, p. 39) affirms that neurosis and psychosis are immaturity, even when appearances are contradictory. Bowen (1960) notes the increasing gap between physical and psychological growth in the developmental history of the schizophrenic. Hill (1955, p. 68) notes the immaturity of schizophrenia; Winder (1960) reviews the psychological studies giving documentation.

The author's conception of the mechanism of self-perpetuation of the behavioral deviations is in sharp contrast to early psychoanalytic models (Fenichel, 1945), which were based on trauma. Munroe (1955) describes the shift from the trauma model to an emphasis on the reactions of the person to the trauma. Weakland (1960) notes that early models emphasized trauma to the neglect of repetitive patterns of experience, which is the author's emphasis. Concepts related to self-perpetuation, in the literature, and the implications of this principle for therapeutic intervention are discussed in the chapter "Therapeutic Process."

The interpretation of all behavioral deviations in terms of experiential deprivation is related to the research and theories that emphasize the importance of general and exploratory experience in the realization of capacity. It is related to the concept of self-actualization, which is affirmed by Rogers (1951), who reviews the literature for similar ideas. Harlow (1953) amply documents the conclusion that monkeys explore and learn independent of any biological drive. Nissen (1954) affirms that a capacity pushes the organism toward its expression and development. Young (1961, pp. 48-56) reviews the studies demonstrating the presence of general activity apart from the organism's effort to satisfy biological needs. The general activity is variously described as playful, manipulative, exploratory and curious. It is viewed as directed toward the realization of capacity and the expression of an activity drive.

Bindra (1961) affirms that spontaneous or general acts are characteristic of an organism's behavior, but consummatory responses, which have been emphasized in research, are infrequent events. The sum of all these studies is to give the knockout blow to reductionism. In the author's view, behavioral deviations have in common the blocking or limiting of spontaneous, playful, exploratory behavior, which is essential to the realization of capacities in normal development. All behavioral deviations are thus experiential deprivations. Experiences are repetitive and cofirmatory rather than new and challenging. Corrective action must be directed toward providing new experiences (before the eyes) rather than sharing experiences (in the head), as Shlien (1961) proposes.

Pious (1961) carefully points out the adverse influence that the looseness of the concept schizophrenia has on efforts to understand this kind of behavior. Many contradictory reports probably result from this looseness. He advocates the solution of definitions that are more operational and empirical than those in current use. Sullivan (1956) expresses dissatisfaction with the concept of schizophrenia; he would exclude the simple type from the category; Winder (1960) attributes contradictory research results to the vagueness of the concept. Psychotic deviation is more rigorously defined than schizophrenia and should assist in obtaining repeatable results.

The description of the developmental histories is from the viewpoint of therapist, not scientist. It is highly selective and thus simplified in order to lay the groundwork for the strategy of therapeutic intervention. Since at the level of method this book deals primarily with the psychotic deviation, the question will now be considered of the correspondence between the development of the psychotic deviation as described here, and of schizophrenia, as described in the literature. Both Arieti (1955) and Hill (1955) summarize their conclusions from broad clinical experience about the development of schizophrenia in their books. Speers and Lansing (1965) provide excellent observations of family relationships made in the course of treating a few schizophrenic children and their mothers. A summary article by Wolman (1965) gives an excellent description of family relationships associated with the development of schizophrenia and provides many references to primary sources. Clausen and Kohn (1960) include studies of a sociological nature. Bowen (1960) briefly reviews the observations made from the special perspective of family therapy. He specifically notes that overt rejection is unusual, which is in accord with the author's view that the essential difference in the development of psychotic deviation and character disorder is one of whether the rejection is overt or subtle.

Arieti (1955, pp. 60-61) specifically notes that in schizophrenic development the mother does not encourage relationships with others and that she blocks the child's relationship to distant relatives and friends. Searles (1965, Ch. 8) notes the mother's injunction against turning to others, which results in an excessive dependence on her.

Generally speaking, the literature confirms that something like what the author describes for the psychotic deviation does occur in the development of schizophrenia. The major objections are likely to be that the author has left out highly significant details and that he has given undue importance to others. For example, Wolman (1965, 1966) gives a similar status to the role reversal between mother and child that the author gives to the failure of the mother to support the development of interpersonal relationships. The author does not question that role reversal is a consistent finding. He does believe that his choice for emphasis is better because it permits the relating of the psychotic deviation to all other developmental deviations, which Wolman's choice does not do. Bowen makes clear that the entire pattern of family relationships is deviant, not merely that between mother and child. The father is an equal participant and contributes to the child's psychosis by his lack of support for the mother and by his emotional divorce from her. Most of the literature referred to above gives the father a similar status of importance in the development of schizophrenia. The author accepts the importance of the pattern of relationships in the entire family. The author's description is aimed at highlighting the mother's failure to support a broadening pattern of interpersonal relationships, upon which he bases his strategy of therapeutic intervention. A more detailed account of the development is helpful in making decisions of methods and techniques, but not for strategic purposes. If strategy changes as with family therapy, then the relative importance of developmental events changes also.

Therapeutic Process: Definitions and Theory

The therapeutic process consists of a series of related interactions that progressively alter the nature of the relationship between therapist and client. The basic data are the totality of interactions from the first hello to the final good-bye. How this totality can be broken down in a way that will assist the therapist in maintaining technical control over the process makes the subject matter for this and the following two chapters. This chapter will introduce the theoretical constructs of the therapeutic process with logical and empirical definitions and take note of the relationships among the constructs. The following two chapters will give further elaboration of the constructs and demonstrate their use in maintaining technical control.

This chapter presents the theory of the general nature of the therapeutic process. The therapist's conceptualizing and decision-making in adapting the therapeutic process to the requirements of a particular client for a specific developmental deviation is called therapeutic programing and the plan he makes is called the therapeutic program. The plan of group therapy presented later in this book is an illustration of a therapeutic program; it presents the author's resolution of the problem of applying the general therapeutic process to the specific case of the psychotic deviation.

Therapeutic potential and gain

The therapeutic process is a functional one; by definition and by agreement between therapist and client it is aimed at assisting the client in overcoming some of the limitations of his developmental history, i.e., aimed at the production of therapeutic gain. All interactions may be regarded from the viewpoint of evaluating their contribution to this objective.

The production of therapeutic gain depends on the quality of the relationship between therapist and client. If the relationship ends, the possibility of therapeutic gain ceases. The relationship may permit the necessary interactions to achieve a certain therapeutic gain or it may block them. The relationship, then, is the tool necessary for the production of therapeutic gain. It must be cared for with the deliberate concern that any good tradesman gives to his tools. An interaction may make the relationship more or less suitable for its therapeutic purpose or it may not affect its suitability. From these considerations the author proposes a functional analysis of all interactions in terms of their influence on 1) the therapeutic potential of the relationship, and 2) the production of therapeutic gain.

The basic nature of therapeutic gain is the same as growth. The construct adds to that of growth the connotation that the change in emotional life took place with the assistance of highly specialized help and with the aid of a carefully controlled interpersonal relationship. Therapeutic gain may be further broken down into the changes of emotional life that broaden the client's potential for interpersonal experience and the changes that represent movement along the developmental scale. Alteration of the way the client structures the relationship to prevent experiences essential to growth represents a therapeutic gain even though no movement along the developmental scale takes place. The change is essential to and is preparatory for such movement along the developmental scale. These kinds of changes in the client will be referred to as preparatory therapeutic gain. For example, a client's suspicion reduces the therapist's power to carry out with him those interactions that are essential to his growth. He keeps his distance from the therapist rather than participating in the search for what is wrong, why it is wrong and how it can be corrected. Interactions that serve the function of reducing this client's suspicion will thus serve the purpose of therapeutic gain even though no movement along the developmental scale takes place. The interactions to reduce his suspicion are prepartory to those that will result in such movement. Therapeutic gains that result in actual movements of the client up the developmental scale will be designated as fulfilling. The construct of fulfilling therapeutic gain is closely related to and highly dependent on that of developmental scale, especially for its empirical definition. It requires reference to the ordering of the changing attributes of behavior with movement toward maturity in order to determine whether fulfilling therapeutic gain has taken place. There is no corresponding systematic theory for the evaluation of preparatory therapeutic gain. It is a gap in present knowledge of the therapeutic process that very much needs to be filled. In the meantime, to identify preparatory therapeutic gains, the therapist must rely on his general knowledge of developmental deviations and his imagination about the way the client's structure of the therapeutic relationship is biasing the client's experience.

Contrasting and substituting

The above considerations explain how the therapist may determine when therapeutic gain takes place. The question now is: How is therapeutic gain produced? It is proposed that there are two main processes, called *contrasting* and *substituting*, that bring about therapeutic gain. By *contrasting* is meant the verbal comparison by therapist and client of attributes of the actual relationship and the client's structure of the relationship. Contrasting is a comparison of inferences that are arrived at by two different means: 1) consideration of all interactions betwen client and therapist up to a particular time to infer the qualities of the actual relationship, and 2) the behavior of the client to infer the client's structure. It is an examination of the client's assumptions about the nature of the relationship which are not justified by the history of interaction. By substituting is meant the attributes of the interactions that give the client information about what he and his relation to the world are like, information that his developmental history either has not provided at all or only incompletely. The information is not interpreted to the client; it is not verbalized. He may draw his own conclusions from the experiences or he may give them no thought.

Substituting is based on the therapist's knowledge and theory.

The therapist arranges for the client to have experiences that he believes will provide the basic material from which the client may grow. The therapist postulates that the client's immaturity is in part based upon his having missed, or having had a distorted form of, a certain class of experiences that is found in the normal developmental sequence. The therapist does not undertake to communicate to the client the theoretical model that he uses in arriving at his decision of what kind of substitute experiences the client needs. He does his theorizing, makes his decisions and builds the substitute experiences into the therapeutic program. Contrasting is much more of a mutual type of interaction. The therapist joins the client in search for a better understanding for the client of the relationship with the therapist. The aim of contrasting then is to improve understanding, which the client can then use to improve his behavior. The aim of substituting is to improve his behavior but not his understanding. Contrasting is a progressive alteration of the client's verbal model of the nature of the relationship, which assists the client in gaining control of the distortions he brings into his relationships. Therapeutic gain through contrasting is mediated by understanding; through substituting, it is direct and unmediated.

It is possible for contrasting to be a special case of substituting. There is no question that experiences like those of contrasting are a part of normal development. The education of the child should assist him to understand when he is expecting too much, too little, when he is too aloof, when he is too intimate and forward and so on. It should assist him to make a verbal model of a relationship that is giving him trouble. When these kinds of experiences have been absent in infancy, the therapist, in deliberately putting them into the therapeutic program, is substituting. In spite of this possible overlap, the two processes may be logically and empirically distinguished. The author believes that making the distinction assists the therapist in conceptualizing the requirements for a therapeutic program and in maintaining technical control of it.

The interactions that serve the function of contrasting also serve that of substituting, but the reverse does not hold. Contrasting takes place in a relationship between therapist and client that is like that of a partnership. The therapist communicates his high regard for the client, his confidence in the client's ability to figure out his problems. He permits considerable latitude to the initiative of the client. These features of the contrasting—those that attribute to the client a relatively high level of power, competence and prestige—serve the function of substituting. It is for the client a kind of relationship that brings new experiences and tends to broaden the perspective acquired during the developmental deviation. This relationship of contrasting to substituting determines much of the form of the technique of contrasting, which will be discussed in the next chapter. It is always essential to the success of the therapeutic program that the therapist continually review the contrasting interactions from the viewpoint of substituting. When using contrasting, the therapist must be continually alert to the possibility that it is taking place in a way to play the client's game. For example, if the client wishes to play a game of being a dependent child who is reassured and taught things, contrasting can take place in a way to reinforce these preferences of the dependent client and thus reinforce his immaturity rather than help overcome it.

Relation to developmental scale. Interactions that serve the function of contrasting and of substituting may be found at every level of the developmental scale to which the therapeutic process is applied. The relative proportions of contrasting and substituting should change greatly as the client moves in the therapeutic process from infancy to adulthood. There will be progressively less substituting; and progressively more contrasting. One of the major problems in working out a therapeutic program is to arrive at the proper proportions of substituting and contrasting. The later chapters dealing with a program of group therapy for the psychotic deviation represent the author's specific solution to this general therapeutic problem. The chapters will show a heavy emphasis on substituting in the beginning phase of therapy; this changes to a heavy emphasis on contrasting when the level of childhood is reached.

Relation to competence of therapist and client. Substituting makes heavy demands on the competence of the therapist; contrasting, on that of the client. Substituting makes no demand on the verbal competence of the client; it does require that he be able to experience the critical abstract attributes of the interaction. (Contrasting is in fact highly dependent on the skill of the therapist, but this is not readily apparent from the appearance of the therapist-client interactions.) Substituting is the means of increasing the competence of the client to a level that permits contrasting and makes it efficient. It is the means of developing an impoverished ego. On the other hand, it is sometimes necessary to do some contrasting before substituting of a particular kind of experience can take place. This is the case when the client is so biased in the way he experiences the interaction that he is not capable of registering the critical attributes. With the suspicious client, for example, it is sometimes necessary to bring out the contrast between his suspicion and the therapist's trustworthy behavior in order to make him capable of experiencing the therapist's trustworthiness. The interactions of the therapist that show trustworthiness cannot substitute for the lack of such experiences in the past until the client is made capable of registering the trustworthiness of the therapist by the process of contrasting. By altering the client's biases and avoidance reactions, contrasting broadens the potential for experience; substituting makes use of this new potential. These considerations reveal that the two processes are highly inter-related, with one process sometimes depending on the other.

Relation to learning theory. The learning paradigm of substituting is concept formation; that of contrasting is discriminatory learning. This view of the two main processes relates them to the sizeable body of psychological knowledge that is available about these types of learning. Substituting provides the client with a larger and larger sample of information about what he and the world are like. It improves his concepts by the addition of information which accrues from the therapist's careful control of the actual relationship so that participation in it will provide experiences not found in the developmental deviation of the client. The new information tends to alter his concepts of self and world.

The process of contrasting is not designed to give new information but to assist the client in learning to be more discriminating and accurate in the interpretation of the information that he already has. For example, if his reaction to all supervisors, including the therapist, is the same, the therapist may invite the client to review his information about supervisors and in particular his information about the therapist as a supervisor. The therapist undertakes to assist the client in making intra-class distinctions and to help him make corresponding discriminatory behavioral reactions. The client should laugh at the supervisor who is an ass, fight with the one who is a tyrant, cooperate with the one who is a leader, who is of genuine assistance and who increases the efficiency of his subordinates. The client must learn to distinguish in his total behavioral response the ass from the tyrant and both of these from the leader.

Conditioned response learning theory provides still another view of the two main therapeutic processes. Substituting is the conditioning of new interpersonal expectations and the extinguishing of old ones. His developmental deviation has taught the client to expect a certain kind of reaction from people when he behaves in a certain way. When the client behaves this way in his relationship to the therapist and the expected reaction does not occur, there is an extinction trial. For example, in the psychotic deviation, acting in accordance with one's feelings is punished by the mother, and acting in accordance with her will and as if one did not have a will of one's own is rewarded. The therapist does not punish the client for his feelings but rather tries to establish rapport with them. The therapist conditions the client to expect reward for expressions of his feelings and extinguishes the old expectation of punishment. From this viewpoint, contrasting corresponds to the holding down of an animal's foot in avoidance conditioning. The animal does not learn that shock no longer follows a signal as long as it consistently raises its foot. In the same way, the avoidance and defensive reactions of the client may prevent him from learning that the old interpersonal expectations are no longer valid. Contrasting is aimed at drawing his attention to the change in his circumstances and pointing out to him that the punishment which used to follow a particular response is not there anymore.

Corresponding distortion processes

Each of the two instruments of therapeutic gain has a distortion, a process that looks like the legitimate one but is in fact invalid. The distortion follows a course very different from that of the legitimate process and consequently leads to a very different outcome. The legitimate process leads to therapeutic gain; the distortion to therapeutic disaster. The therapist must be very familiar with the distortions in order to insure that he can differentiate them from the legitimate therapeutic processes.

The distortion of substituting is in essence that the interactions between therapist and client have the same quality as those of the client's developmental deviation. When this happens, the interactions have no power to substitute for the client's experiential deprivations. The experience with the therapist confirms his present view of himself and the world. The therapist takes the role of the significant people in the client's life and behaves toward the client in much the same way as these significant people have done and perhaps still do.

It might at first seem to be a highly improbable coincidence that the therapist would respond to the client in the same way as other significant people have done in his past. But this is not the case. It is a curious but profound principle that the client's behavior forms a stimulus that tends to elicit the very responses that he has most frequently met in his developmental deviation. The most direct and natural responses to the client are likely to be the very ones that have made therapy necessary for him. As a result of being treated in a particular way, a person learns to behave in ways that are likely to continue to elicit that treatment. If he is treated with love and respect, he learns to show friendship, affection and positive regard for others to which they tend to respond with love. If he is treated with contempt, he tends to learn responses of subtle fighting, which tends to elicit contempt from people. This is the basic principle of the self-perpetuation of developmental deviations. It is the truth of the Golden Rule, a truth that is usually missed in interpreting the Golden Rule as a duty. In effect, the client continues to insist that others must change their behavior toward him and then he will change his; in therapy he must learn to change his behavior first, which will in turn change other people's behavior toward him. If the therapist participates in this self-perpetuating mechanism, he distorts the process of substituting and reduces the therapeutic potential of the relationship to zero.

A special case of the distortion of substituting, which deserves emphasis, is that which occurs when the therapeutic program emphasizes contrasting. Full attention to the features of the interaction that contribute to the contrasting results in a neglect of the question of whether the contrasting is carried out in a way that gives the client experiences like those of his developmental deviation or experiences that are more like those found in normal development. This distortion is probably responsible for a large percentage of therapeutic failures. It is expecially likely to occur if a therapist conceives of the therapeutic process as entirely one of contrasting and does not recognize the process of substituting.

The distortion of contrasting is revealed by the observation that the client is building a more and more complete and accurate verbal model of his interpersonal difficulties but that he is making no corresponding changes in his behavior. He learns to talk with ease about his troubles but he does not learn to behave more maturely. The distortion of contrasting is most likely to occur when 1) the therapist places a high value on verbal and intellectual processes and tends to neglect other kinds of behavior; the therapist judges a person more by what he says than what he does, and 2) the therapist fails to confine the content of contrasting to the client's developmental level; he uses contrasting to show the client things that developmentally he is not prepared to understand or assimilate; the therapist fails to consider the readiness of the client.

The avoidance of the distortion of contrasting depends on the selection and training of therapists. The process of contrasting is properly applied when it is used to assist the client in making a behavioral change. A change in what he thinks or the way he verbalizes his problem is merely a means to an end, not an end in itself. Intellectualism on the part of the therapist is associated with the loss of this perspective and the treating of a change in what the client says about his problem as evidence of therapeutic gain. The application of contrasting to content outside the range of the client's developmental level is coercive and forces a pseudogrowth, of which the glibness about interpersonal difficulties is one manifestation. Progress along the developmental scale is gradual and orderly, with the present phase dependent on each one preceding it. There is no way that a client in late infancy can profitably apply himself to the problems of adolescence or adulthood. If the therapist uses contrasting to show such a client his shortcomings as an adolescent or adult, the information is not informative but coercive in the same way that a teacher's calling a child a "big boy" is. The teacher is really saying either you behave in a certain way or you are not a big boy. Contrasting, properly applied, reveals to the client matters that are of immediate relevance and emotional significance to him, aspects of his emotional life that he is now ready to alter.

Implication for unit of analysis and criterion of therapeutic gain

The use of contrasting and substituting in the achievement of therapeutic gain requires careful control of the present and immediate relationship between therapist and client. The therapist will be most precise in his technical control of the therapeutic process if he never undertakes an analysis of the therapeutic interaction in terms other than those of the relationship. The focus on the therapist-client relationship is fundamental; it determines relevance and emphasis and meaning. The interaction between therapist and client, like any interpersonal process, is extremely complex and provides many other possibilities of focus. There are the symptoms of the client, his report of his relationship to significant people such as mother, wife and children, and his report of the ideas and feelings that go on in his head.

It is the grossest of errors to focus on the symptoms of the client. The symptoms are far removed from the problems that are producing them. The client himself is very eager to talk about his symptoms and the therapist will not escape from his subject. The client tends to feel that if he just tells the therapist enough about his symptoms, the therapist will do something about them. There is a tendency for the client to become dependent on the therapist and to wish to perpetuate the relationship. If the therapist shows an interest in the symptoms, the client will believe that he must perpetuate his symptoms in order to keep the therapist from ending the sessions. Since there is a limit to how long one can talk about the ordinary symptoms, if these become the focus of therapy, the client must give his symptoms considerable elaboration. Finally, talk about symptoms does not give to the therapist the slightest hint about how to control the processes of substituting and contrasting. It diverts his attention from these important processes and usually leads to therapeutic failure. On the other hand, if the focus of the therapist is on the relationship, he will be thinking about such questions as the following when the client is talking about his symptoms: Is he telling me that he does not feel like facing up to responsibility? Does he wish to be excused from wrongdoing because he is ill? Is he defining himself as the weak person and me as the strong person? Is he justifying dependency demands which will be forthcoming? Is he challenging me, that is, does he wish to demonstrate that he knows more about symptoms than I do? Does he wish to show how strong he is by picturing how much he has accomplished in spite of such handicaps? The client's symptoms, like anything else that he brings up, are of interest in therapy only insofar as they reveal the relationship between therapist and client.

A focus on symptoms is but a special case of a perspective that attributes everything that happens in therapy to the client's illness, personality deficiencies or idiosyncrasies. Such a view of the client as a pre-set robot is inimical to therapeutic gain. However loosely or symbolically or even inappropriately, the client's behavior responds to the behavior of the therapist; it demonstrates the client's understanding and structuring of the therapeutic relationship. It is impossible to evaluate what the client does in any therapeutically meaningful way without reference to what the therapist does. The therapeutic process should give to the client a clearer understanding of the relation between his behavior and what other people do. This is not likely to happen if the therapist sees no relationship between what the client does and what he himself does. The therapist is one of the two protagonists in therapy. To be effective in his work the therapist must not be client centered; his focus must be on client in relation to therapist.

Control of contrasting and substituting to achieve therapeutic gain may require that the therapist explore with the client his relationships to significant people in his life. The therapist would do well to keep in mind that these relationships are not of interest in and for themselves, but only to the extent that they contribute to a more exact application of the therapeutic relationship to the achievement of therapeutic gain. If the therapist keeps the perspective in mind, he will not lose himself and the client in the exploration of these relationships. He will spare himself the troublesome problem of the reliability of the client's report of these relationships—the correspondence between what the client says and what actually is or was taking place in these relationships. How and what the client reports about these relationships is of significance for the interpretation of the therapeutic relationship, apart from any considerations of reliability.

This perspective will also prevent the therapeutic interaction from clarifying the historical development of the client without revealing the relation between history and present circumstances. The perspective recommends the exploration of historical relationships to the extent that it clarifies the therapeutic relationship. An exploration of history for its own sake encourages the client in his avoidance of responsibility for corrective action on his developmental deficiencies. It tends to provide the client with excuses rather than increased understanding of how to go about solving his current problems. The verbal elaboration of historical relationships and of emotionally traumatic interpersonal events in the client's life are neither necessary nor sufficient for therapeutic gain. When emotional release could not take place in the past because of the structure of the relationship in which the trauma occurred and has not taken place in the intervening time because of the way the client structures his relationships, corrective action is not a matter of releasing the emotions but of altering the way the client structures his current relationships. The client must learn to structure relationships in a way that permits rather than blocks emotional expressions. If the therapist values catharsis and clarity of historical relationships in and for themselves, he is likely to be misled into believing therapeutic gain is taking place when in fact it is not. Neither catharsis nor elaboration of historical relationships insures that therapeutic gain is taking place, just as

an increasingly accurate verbal model of one's current relationships does not do so. The ultimate criterion of therapeutic gain is
whether the therapist-client relationship is changing in the direction of increasing maturity, and this deserves the therapist's continuing review.

Discussion and references

The distinction between the doing or practice and the conceptualization of therapy must be kept in mind in the examination and
evaluation of the literature about it. In a famous study, Fiedler
(1950) discovered that experienced therapists of different theoretical conviction were more alike in what they actually did during
the therapy sessions than were beginning therapists of the same
school. Alexander (1963) points out that psychoanalytic practice
does not always follow theory and Marks et al. (1966) conclude
the same is true of the more rigorous behavior therapy. Berger
et al. (1966) insist that results of behavior therapy cannot be attributed to the theory because many things are done that are not
represented in the theory. A lack of exact correspondence between
practice and theory is found among all approaches. The doing of
therapy can proceed on entirely empirical grounds. This approach
merely requires the observation that certain actions of the therapist toward clients who have certain kinds of behavior problems
produce results that are desired. Much of the practice of therapy
appears to proceed on these grounds. Freeman (1965) defends the
empirical approach. Klapman (1959) reports that Marsh built an
enthusiastic program of group therapy for psychotic patients with
no other theory than that of stimulating and inspiring them toward a happier state of mind. When Rosen (1964) insists that the
therapist must be a substitute parent to the schizophrenic, he is
giving instructions for the doing of therapy. He offers no conceptualization of this practice. It is possible to appreciate what is done
by a therapist while rejecting his conceptualization of what he
has done; it is a matter of doing the same things for different
reasons. For example, the author feels close to Adler in the practice of therapy, but very distant from him in its conceptualization.

    Excluding existentialism, there are three major systems of

theory about therapy: the psychoanalytic, the nondirective or client-centered and the behavioristic. Psychoanalytic theory is encyclopedically summarized in Fenichel (1945) and imaginatively interpreted for the layman by Munroe (1955). Munroe in comparing the classical, Freudian or libido analysts with the Neo-Freudian, non-libido analysts gives a good picture of the range of practice and thought within these groups. Munroe makes the distinction described above: The classical analyst may act like a Neo-Freudian, as for example, Alexander, and Neo-Freudians may retain more of classical psychoanalysis in their procedures than in their reports of them. The nondirective, client-centered approach and the changes in it over the years are authoritatively reported in the publications of Rogers (1942, 1951). There appears to be much less variation among the therapists using this approach than among the psychoanalysts. The behavior therapy, or modification theory and practice, is reported in such publications as those by Jacobson (1938), Wolpe (1958), Eysenck (1960), and Ullmann and Krasner (1965, 1966). Eysenck compares behavior therapy and psychoanalysis and very much favors the former. Grossberg (1964) and Rackman (1965) review validating studies of behavior therapy and conclude that the behavioral approach is promising. A summary of the position of the behavior modification group on the issues of therapy, as these are revealed in the conception of the role of the therapist, is presented by Krasner (1966).

Comparison of the systems of therapy is presented by Frank (1961), Ford and Urban (1963) and Munroe (1955) from distinctive viewpoints and with differences in scope. Frank emphasizes the similarity among systems that is found in the common use of persuasion. Munroe considers only the within-group differences of psychoanalysts. Ford and Urban compare ten therapists, who represent diverse conceptualizations of therapy, in terms of how each conceives of the normal course of behavior development, the development of behavior disorder, the goals of therapy and how change is brought about and evaluated. From the comparison, they offer specific recommendations for both system-building and the shaping of research to evaluate a system. The discussion of issues among therapists by Munroe and Ford and Urban reassures the author that he has taken a position on all key issues, which is

important for any system-builder. His position on most issues is
inferrable from the definition of constructs and the theory of their
interrelationships.

With wide variation in conceptualization and even wider variation in practice, comparison of the theory presented in this
chapter with other theories and discussion of the question of its
agreement and disagreement with current practice of therapy
would be a big undertaking in itself. For the present, the author
will present some of the major characteristics of his theory and
make brief reference to the literature to permit perspective.

The author's constructs are at a relatively low level of abstraction, and all are at the same homogeneous level, which permits
excellent interlocking among them. What is wrong with the client
is described in terms of how he avoids interaction and how he
patterns it. What is wrong is also viewed as a difference between
the pattern of interpersonal relationship in which the client has
participated in his development and the progressive alteration of
pattern of relationship with movement along the developmental
scale. Substituting refers to the actions of the therapist viewed in
the perspective of this difference, which defines social deprivation.
How change is brought about is described in terms of kinds of
interaction between therapist and client. The measurement of
change is in terms of altered patterns of interaction viewed in the
perspective of the orderly sequence of such changing patterns
along the developmental scale. In contrast to this homogeneity,
psychoanalytic theory conceives of what is wrong and how it is
corrected in terms of intrapsychic and therefore intervening variables (Tolman, 1951). Kind of interaction between parent and
child or therapist and patient is elevated to a higher level of
abstraction by inferring its influence on the relationship among
id, ego, superego and reality. The nondirective system similarly
elevates the level of abstraction by relating interaction to the
client's perceptual field. As Krasner (1966) and Grossberg (1964)
note, the behavior modifiers are divided on this question. Those
who follow the learning theory of Hull (1943), such as Wolpe and
Eysenck, use intervening variables; those who follow the position
of Skinner (1938, 1953, 1957) do not. Thus, in this respect the
author's theory is Skinnerian. A homogeneous and relatively low

level of abstraction permits a closer, more obvious relationship between the conception of what is wrong and the corrective action of the therapist than is possible for those theories that have a heterogeneous and high level of abstraction. The author's constructs refer to overt acts which are public, observable, objective events. The advantages of these features for verification are great.

In the author's view, the therapeutic process is the same in its essential nature for the entire range, which is represented, at the theoretical level, by the applicability of contrasting and substituting and by the same criterion of therapeutic gain, i.e., movement along the developmental scale. A difference of method and technique is indicated not only with change from psychotic to neurotic to character disorder deviation, but also within the course of the therapeutic process for any one of these deviations. Classical analysts, nondirective therapists and behavior modifiers all propose a uniform method of therapy. The Neo-Freudians, notably Sullivan (1956), propose a practice of adaptation of the method to the nature of the disorder, but offer no uniform conceptualization of the practice. Alexander (1948, 1963), while Freudian, is a reformer and an untiring advocate of a flexible method. The author's view of the features of the interaction that are essential for therapeutic gain parallels Alexander's description of the requirements for corrective emotional experience, especially the description in his recent publication. As is well known, Freud questioned the applicability of his method to schizophrenia; he never conceptualized that broad a range of therapy. Rogers (1961) affirms that the conditions required for therapy are the same for neurotic, normal and schizophrenic individuals. By conditions he means attitudes of the therapist. The author disagrees; the therapist must use different actions (attitudes) in order to stimulate the growth of clients at diverse developmental levels. The behavior modifiers propose a uniform role for the therapist, but a diversification of techniques (Grossberg, 1964) in manipulating the conditions governing learning. Hill (1955, Chapter VIII) regards psychotherapy with schizophrenics as a special case of psychotherapy in general. With this, the author agrees, but it must be emphasized that the sameness is not in method or technique. Dawson (1961, pp. 118-122) cautions against the application to schizophrenic patients of psychotherapeutic methods that have developed from psychoanalytic treatment of the neurotic without validation of their effectiveness with schizophrenics. He advocates the development of techniques that are specifically designed for the treatment of the schizophrenic. Pious (1961) gives a similar warning. Ford and Urban (1963) recommend that system-builders move in the direction of proposing specific treatments for specific disorders. The author's theory gives the broad outline for a systematic change of method within and between developmental deviations. The detailed description and final decisions regarding content (method and technique) of therapeutic program is left to be written in by empirical research.

The author's guiding principle for shaping method, which is a changing emphasis from substituting to contrasting with movement up the developmental scale, has massive support in the literature, as the author interprets it. Those therapists who have worked primarily at the upper levels of the developmental scale, as did Freud, are most insistent on a model of therapy most like that of contrasting. Those whose work has included much experience with disorders low on the developmental scale, such as Sullivan with schizophrenics and Alexander with psychosomatic disorders, have tended to insist on both fuller participation and a carefully specified quality of participation. Those who have worked successfully with schizophrenics (Brody and Redlich, 1952; Rosen, 1953; Hill, 1955; Arieti, 1955; Sehekaye, 1956; Burton, 1961; Dawson et al., 1961; Boszormenyi-Nagy and Framo, 1965; Searles, 1965) are in general agreement about the requirement for the full participation of the therapist. Boszormenyi-Nagy (1965) specifically affirms that the relational component of therapy becomes greater as the patient's ego weakness increases. Klapman (1959) organizes his book in terms of methods that are optimally applicable to minimally, moderately and severely disorganized personality states, which implicity observes the organization of the author's guideline. Ruesch (1955) proposes that nonverbal elements of therapy are of most importance in severe disturbance, which gradually shifts to a verbal emphasis as the disturbance becomes less severe. The construct of substituting is empirically but not logically related to that of metacommunication (Ruesch and Bateson, 1951).

Framo (1965) observes that many therapists believe the critical aspects of therapy are nonverbal. Hollon (1966) specifies that for borderline states the therapeutic interaction must recapitulate the quality of interaction between mother-child in healthy development. All of these reports from the literature give support to the concept of substituting as a legitimate and essential therapeutic force, worthy of full conceptual recognition, as well as to the proposed relationship between it and contrasting.

The author would like to gratefully acknowledge the influence of Sullivan's construct (1953, 1954, 1956) of parataxic mode of experience on the development of the construct of contrasting and of the description by Allen (1942) of his therapeutic contact with children on the development of the construct of substituting.

Munroe (1955, p. 510) suggests that only recently has the value of mixing insight, experience-with-the-therapist, encouragement, and direct help, as proposed by Adler, come to be appreciated. Even so, the literature referred to above shows that it has long been practiced by successful therapists, especially those who work with behavior deviations low on the developmental scale. This chapter then offers a formal conceptualization of an old and general practice that has finally come to be appreciated.

The concept of distortion of substituting is a new way of conceptualizing an old problem. In psychoanalytic literature it is discussed in terms of countertransference or the therapist's acting out rather than analyzing the patient's problems. In nondirective theory it would presumably be the failure of the therapist to give unconditional positive regard. Behavior modification has no conception of it, possibly because it does not occur in a relationship in which the therapist has such a definite role. The concept is related to the vicious circles of Horney (1937). Krasner (1966) notes that the behavior modifiers are concerned with what reinforces the behavior in the present situation. The idea of the distortion of substituting is that the client's behavior elicits behavior from others that maintains his own. In *experience 6*, Bion (1961) observes that the act of interpreting may reinforce the basic culture of dependency and in *experience 7* that the leader may be manipulated into playing a part in someone else's fantasy. In the author's terms, both would be instances of the distortion of substituting. Cohen (1952) describes how the schizophrenic manipulates the therapist into being like the adults in his early life. Secord and Backman (1961) carefully develop the thesis that exposure to a social environment that is incongruous to beliefs is essential to behavioral change. McReynolds (1960) deduces that the theory of cognitive dissonance requires a therapeutic program for schizophrenics of exposure to new and different experiences of a kind and at a rate that can be assimilated.

Similarly the distortion of contrasting is a new conception of an old problem. Freud early concluded that the recovery of repressed memories without the repressed emotion was fruitless. The problem is frequently discussed in terms of intellectual without emotional insight. It is related to a change by Rogers (1948 compared to 1951) from an emphasis of technique to one of the attitude of the therapist toward the client. In the author's view, Rogers' observation that the same techniques carried out with different attitudes produce unreliable results represents an empirical demonstration of the distortion of contrasting and of the importance of substituting.

In its emphasis on the present and immediate relationship, the author's theory is least like classical psychoanalysis and most like behavior modification. Neo-Freudian theory occupies an intermediate position. Again practice is not in accord with conceptualization, and Alexander is an exception. Hill (1955, p. 146) finds that psychoanalysts who work with schizophrenics prefer to deal with current problems rather than with infantile memories or dreams or fantasy.

Symptoms are viewed as one aspect among many of the client's pattern of relationship to people; they are not singled out for special consideration, which is decidedly different from both psychoanalysis and behavior modification. Symptoms are not given special consideration in client-centered therapy, but for a vastly different reason from that of the author: the method is believed to be applicable to all symptoms.

A significant feature of the author's theory is the specification of the criteria of therapeutic gain. The specification has both logical clarity and exact reference to observable events. Thus the constructs can easily be given operational meaning (Bergmann and Spence, 1951). No other system of therapy has this quality, except that of the behavior modifiers of the Skinnerian line. Ford and Urban (1963, p. 689) specifically note that all of the systems they compare are alike in conceptualizing therapy in terms of subjectively observable responses and that this feature of the theories makes a problem for verification that has not yet been solved.

Most of the systems of therapy give major emphasis to what the author describes as preparatory therapeutic gains. For example, Rogers (1961) specifies an increasing self-acceptance, perceptual accuracy, openness to experience and personal integration as indices of therapeutic gain. All of these the author would regard as preparatory to the big event, movement along the developmental scale. Rogers also mentions that behavior will be more mature.

There is widespread agreement that the proper criterion of therapeutic gain is a change in the way of acting, in total behavior, and not merely a change in verbal behavior. Dreikurs (1963) insists on the criterion of change of life style; he rejects insight as a basic or even a prerequisite of cure. Ackerman (1963) points out that therapeutic change is not merely an increased awareness or release of unconscious urges but an increased potential for fulfillment. Foulkes and Anthony (1957, p. 242) propose that a change in the person is indicated both first and best in his interaction with others. Rosen (1964) aggressively affirms that a change in the individual toward increased maturity must take place during therapy, or the purpose of therapy is defeated. He clearly differentiates the objective of science to know all and that of therapy to produce increased maturity. The author would like to persuade researchers in this area that no better criterion of therapeutic gain can be proposed than that the pattern of the client's interaction with people changes to one that is higher on the developmental scale.

Therapeutic Potential

The therapist has two aims in his relationship with the client: (1) increasing therapeutic potential, and (2) producing therapeutic gain. Since the second goal is dependent on the first, the therapist, first and foremost, must direct his attention and action at increasing the therapeutic potential. The need for this priority is readily apparent in the extreme instance: the client discontinues his interaction with the therapist; the therapeutic potential drops to zero; all opportunity for producing therapeutic gain is lost. It is less readily apparent when interaction continues, as in the distortion of substituting; here, too, the therapeutic potential drops to zero and no therapeutic gain can be produced.

The concern for therapeutic potential is greatest in the beginning phase when the therapist is doing what is commonly called forming a relationship. Often in these initial interactions the battle for therapeutic gain is won or lost. Some therapists, most likely beginning ones, are so eager to form a relationship that they do so on terms that forever destroy any therapeutic potential. Other therapists are so eager to influence the client toward maturity that they bring pressures to bear on him that are beyond his ability to withstand; unwittingly they drive the client out of the relationship.

Actions related to therapeutic potential are frequently viewed as preliminary, and unskilled therapists tend to be impatient with them. They do not adequately appreciate the critical significance of these preliminary interactions. Yet, to be effective a therapist must carefully lay the appropriate foundation for the therapeutic process itself, and he must become reconciled to this necessity.

The concept of therapeutic potential is a convenient way of

60

referring to the degree to which the relationship supports the therapeutic processes of substituting and contrasting and also the efficiency with which these processes may be executed. If the therapist takes actions which frighten the client into terminating the relationship, the therapeutic potential was not adequate for those particular actions. If the therapist wishes to show to the client the extremity of his dependence on the therapist, he may be unable to do so because of the client's argumentative, challenging and defiant tendencies; the therapeutic potential of the relationship would be adequate only after the preliminary problem of defiance had been solved. If the therapist undertakes to communicate material of therapeutic relevance to a client who is distracted and inattentive, he must work hard and long as compared to communicating the same material to a client who is interested and attentive; thus actions that improve the interest and attention of the client in the interaction improve the efficiency with which the relationship produces therapeutic gain.

It is the therapist's careful, deliberate concern with therapeutic potential that distinguishes the therapeutic relationship from all others. The therapeutic relationship is not the only one that produces growth. Many relationships, the parent-child and teacher-child, for example, support and promote growth, but the therapeutic relationship alone 1) is created for the specific and single purpose of promoting growth; 2) is repeatedly and continuously reviewed in terms of its potential for promoting growth, and 3) is continuously altered to better fulfill the purpose of promoting growth. It is this deliberate control of therapeutic potential that makes the therapeutic relationship alone adequate to serve the purpose of correcting developmental deviations. Other social relationships—friendships, marital and business relationships—tend to be formed between people who wish to participate in a relationship that fits the patterns of the client's emotional life.

Thus if the person prefers a pre-adolescent relationship, he finds friends, business associates and a wife who will relate to him according to the pre-adolescent pattern. In such relationships the participants act out the preferred pattern, re-enforce and strengthen it. No participant has responsibility for a review of the relationship in terms of its power to produce growth.

The first and most critical step in the control of therapeutic potential is for the therapist to accept full and inalienable responsibility. He cannot delegate this responsibility to the client. He must interact with the client in the full consciousness of this responsibility. He must continually evaluate his actions, his approach, his choice of techniques, his total contact with the client in the light of this responsibility. It is understandable and forgivable that he makes mistakes in the exercise of his responsibility; it is neither understandable nor forgivable that he does not accept the responsibility.

In the author's view the control of therapeutic potential requires that the therapist 1) observe the proper priority in focusing on content of interaction, and 2) conform all his actions to certain specifiable values and beliefs.

*Priority of content
influences therapeutic potential*

The more closely related a content area is to therapeutic potential the higher must be the priority given to it. Content related to the four areas listed below must be given a priority over that related to the basic therapeutic processes. Only when the problems presented by these areas of content are adequately resolved does the therapist proceed with the pursuit of therapeutic gain. The four content areas are discussed in the order of decreasing priority.

1) *Continuity and stability of relationship.* Top priority belongs to the handling of material that relates to the continuity or stability of the relationship. This priority is almost automatic in all kinds of relationships. If a child decides he intends to drop out of school, his decision is given priority over his skill in conjugating verbs. If a wife threatens to leave the husband, he drops the question of what the family is having for supper. In the same way the therapist must maintain the continuity of his relationship to the client until it has served its purpose, and the client no longer needs it.

The high priority of this problem does not, however, mean that the therapist must continue the relationship on any terms. A therapeutic relationship above all else must be therapeutic; if it is not, it is nothing. Sometimes it is impossible to maintain the continuity of the relationship without destroying its therapeutic potential. The client simply may not participate in a relationship that has therapeutic potential. The interaction should be continued only until it has been carefully determined that the client will not accept a therapeutic relationship. Termination at that point is better than the perpetuation of interaction that is powerless to bring about growth. Termination, at least, destroys the myth that the client is in therapy. It avoids the discrediting of the value of therapy. The door is left open for him to return when he will accept and participate in a relationship that can help him.

The stability of the relationship requires that the realistic conditions under which the therapist and client meet do not produce excessive threat or stress for the client; they must be satisfactory to him. The client should be given all the information that he requests and needs to know about when, where and at what cost he will meet with the therapist. Any negative attitudes that he has about these realistic conditions should be carefully gone into and, if possible, resolved. For example, the client may be fearful that the neighbors will think he is "crazy" if he continues the relationship with the therapist. There are many ways in which the therapist may reassure the client on this point. The neighbors need not know. Or he can show them how unreasonable it is to think less of him because he is trying to get the help he needs; most people can at some time in their life use special psychological assistance. Similarly, the therapist must help the client work through any feelings of resentment, burden or threat that the cost of the sessions may cause. The client may be fearful of his ability to pay for the sessions. The reality of such a fear must be carefully considered with the client. The client may resent the charges. He may feel the therapist is not being fair and that he is being taken advantage of. The therapist should invite full expression of all such feelings. Finally the client usually has some questions about the therapist's qualifications; these should be answered honestly, straighforwardly, simply and promptly.

Another important area for the stability of the relationship is the relating of the client's problems and aspirations, as he sees them, to the therapeutic sessions. This problem of making the therapeutic program meaningful to the client receives detailed attention in chapters which present the therapeutic program for the psychotic deviation. In essence, the therapist is pointing out to the client the specific possibilities which the therapeutic relationship offers for working out the problems that the client may bring up. If the client sees how he may benefit in specific rather than general terms, he is more likely to continue the sessions than if he cannot. It should not be left entirely to the client to make his own guesses about how he may benefit; the therapist should guide the client.

Any *negative* feelings that the client has toward the therapist or the relationship should be carefully explored in the interest of stability. The principle that negative feelings have priority over positive ones is perhaps similar to Freud's recognition that the therapist should deal with negative transference immediately upon its appearance but might delay dealing with positive transference until late in the course of therapy. One difference is that the author would not pre-judge the negative feelings as transference. There is the possibility that the therapist's arrangement with the client or his attitude toward him is responsible for the negative feelings. Since the ultimate effect of negative feelings is to discontinue the relationship, the therapist must explore these feelings before they reach this point or he loses all opportunity to bring them under control.

The therapist need not limit his attention to hostility that is already present. He can anticipate that certain attitudes of the client will inevitably produce disillusionment and anger. The client's unrealistic expectations are especially likely to generate negative feelings and therefore warrant careful exploration.

2) *Emotional disturbance.* The content of the interaction is associated with different degrees of emotional disturbance, which is manifested by restlessness, inattentiveness, sudden intensity of talking, perspiration, all kinds of discomfort and so on. Some content assists the client in reducing the emotional disturbance; other content elevates the indices of disturbance. As the emotional disturbance increases, the risk of the client's discontinuing the relationship goes up. Also, if the level of emotional disturbance rises to the point that the client experiences the total relationship as

threatening, it destroys the potential of the relationship to reassure the client and to support his growth. On the other hand, if the interaction produces no emotional disturbance in that it deals only with matters that do not threaten the client, it becomes irrelevant to the problem of helping the client overcome the disturbance that some material does have for him. The therapist can control the level of emotional disturbance by focusing on disturbing material when the level of emotional disturbance is low and by permitting the client to escape from such material (and even assisting him by focusing on reassuring material) when the level of disturbance is high.

One special case of the general therapeutic problem of controlling emotional disturbance is the sudden drop of disturbance which frequently occurs after only a few sessions. This is what has been called the "transference cure." In the author's experience, its failure to occur indicates the death of therapy. It seems to mean that the client's experiences with people have been so universally unpleasant that he cannot perceive the therapist as a symbol of hope. Against such background the therapist has no power to support and reassure the client emotionally. Without this reassurance the client seems never to gain the courage to look at himself and his relations with people. The author has never had a client discontinue therapy because of this initial improvement, the significance of which may, however, require special explanation to the client. In order to elevate the emotional disturbance the therapist may then focus on those problems that made necessary the relationship.

3) *Biases of communication.* The exchange of messages between therapist and client is central and vital to the therapeutic processes; any increase in the efficiency and accuracy of communication improves the therapeutic potential of the relationship. Some of the client's biases are so much a part of his developmental deviation that their complete removal depends upon the results of the total therapeutic process. Other biases of communication are less deeply rooted and thus more modifiable. Even if the bias cannot be removed, it can be identified and, in this way, its operation in the therapeutic relationship can be reduced and compensated for by the client. It is a matter of judgment of the therapist as to how

much attention and effort to give to biases of communication at any particular time. On the one hand, he needs to be aware of the rich reward in the increase in therapeutic potential which can be obtained by modifying these biases. On the other hand, he must not push the modification beyond the limitations imposed by the level of the emotional life of the client.

Every developmental level has its characteristic biases of communication which can be modified only to a limited extent unless the client moves to a higher level. At the infantile level, what is said is of little significance compared to non-verbal communication —posturing of body, tone of voice, pattern of movements and gestures. At the childhood level the bias is in the direction of interpreting what is said by an authority figure to be final, ultimate, definitive, unquestionable. There is a poor grasp of the many ways in which a message may be interpreted. A passing, impulsive thought is not well differentiated from a command. A tentative summary of the present understanding of a problem is confused with a final conclusion. At the childhood level, the therapist's efforts to broaden the client's view of a problem is made difficult by the bias of interpreting all of the therapist's actions as advice; the client's set becomes one of discovering subtle and hidden ways he thinks the therapist is using in advising him. The therapist must bring such a bias to the attention of the client but, again, he cannot hope to remove it completely except through the movement of the client to another emotional level. When the client moves on to pre-adolescence, he is more likely to perceive the therapist's actions as alien and potentially hostile to his peer-derived values. Focus on the bias as a matter for discussion makes the client more aware of it and able to compensate to a limited extent for it; movement up the developmental scale ends the bias.

The biases of communication to which the therapist may most profitably apply his actions are those associated with the client's failing efforts to maintain his self-respect. His low self-respect produces a bias of tending to interpret the therapist's messages as condemning, critical or at least uncomplimentary of him. The therapist may contrast the client's bias with his non-judgmental, fact-finding efforts. The client's distrust or suspicion of the therapist, which may be viewed as defensive efforts, results in expressive as well as receptive biases of communication. Out of fear or in anticipation of the therapist's treachery, the client does not communicate his more personal and less worthy thoughts and feelings. He tends to look for and find hidden meanings, which are far removed from those intended by the therapist.

The therapeutic processes of substituting and contrasting are applicable to the modification of these biases. From another viewpoint, which does not consider the effect on the efficiency of the relationship, the resulting changes are preparatory therapeutic gains.

4) *Dominating motives of the client.* The therapist may explain to the client that the purpose of the relationship is to assist him in understanding more clearly how he does relate to people and in learning more effective and satisfying ways of doing so. The therapist must not assume that the client will then be capable of pursuing this objective. Even the skilled therapist with many years of training and experience may be sidetracked by some spurious motive. He will, however, be capable of getting back on the main track and over the long run steadfastly pursue the therapeutic objective. The client is frequently derailed by motives which compete with the therapeutic objective and which completely destroy the therapeutic potential of the relationship unless they are made the focus of attention and altered by the interaction.

The content of such competing motives varies widely among clients and changes many times during the course of working with a single client. The dominating motives have in common the fact that they change the purpose of the therapeutic relationship from one of emotional development to one of satisfying a powerful social motive of the client. The motive may be identified in general terms, as the wish for self-justification, or in such specific terms, as the wish to have the therapist render the judgment that the client is innocent and that his wife is all to blame. It takes very little imagination to see how the domination of this motive in the behavior of the client would destroy all possibility of progress toward the therapeutic objective. The client's report is preoccupied with his wife's failings. In the interest of showing how clean he is of any blame, he neglects to take notice of how what he has done and is doing contributes to the situation in which he finds himself. He is like a lawyer arguing a case to a jury. It is most unlikely that the playing of this role will result in his discovering anything at all about his pattern of interpersonal relationship.

Another interfering dominating motive which is very frequent is the wish for the therapist's approval. A special instance of this occurs in groups functioning at the childhood and pre-adolescent levels. The total interactional pattern of the group becomes in essence one of all of the members yelling to the therapist, "Hey, look at me!" Other interfering motives are of a competitive nature. The client undertakes to show that he knows as much or more about psychological, therapeutic and behavioral problems as the therapist. Or the competition may be manifest in the client's determination not to be influenced by the therapist. He wishes to show his power and independence of will by defeating what he conceives to be the therapist's objective of changing his behavior. He wishes to reduce the therapist to powerlessness by defeating the therapeutic objective.

There are four ways of conceptualizing the mechanism by which dominating motives reduce the therapeutic potential of the relationship. *First,* the dominating motive limits the range of the client's actions to those that serve the motive. The actions which serve the aim of the dominating motive are not at all identical to those actions which would best serve the therapeutic objective. *Second,* the operation of a dominating motive means that the client is not intentionally trying to learn how to relate more effectively to people. For that matter, he is not set to learn at all but to fulfill a social motive. This reduces the efficiency of the interaction for the achieving of therapeutic gain to a level of incidental learning—which is very inefficient compared to purposeful learning. *Third,* and perhaps most definitely, the operation of the dominating motive makes it impossible to carry out the therapeutic processes of substituting and contrasting. When the client is behaving under the influence of a dominating motive, he perceives the actions of the therapist in terms of whether those actions satisfy or frustrate his social motive. Thus, actions of the therapist that could have a substitutive value are neglected by the client, or they frustrate him because they do not satisfy his motive. The client who wishes to be judged innocent finds the therapist's non-judgmental policy frustrating. The therapist may intend such actions to substitute for judgments in the client's developmental history that were too frequent and too critical. But the client does not gain this substitute experience, according to plan; instead he is frustrated because the therapist withholds a judgment of his innocence. The therapist must thus shift his attention from the process of substituting to that of handling the dominating motive of the client. With this resolved and the therapeutic potential of the relationship restored, he may then apply the process of substituting. The process of contrasting fares no better from the interference of dominating motives. Contrasting is a task requiring abstract and conceptual thinking. To carry out the task requires careful and prolonged attention. It requires an interpretation of the interaction not a mere decision as to whether the interaction is or is not satisfying the client's motive. *Fourth,* the unresolved operation of a dominating motive produces much dissatisfaction; the therapist is frustrating the client. It thus moves the client toward ending his participation. The increasing probability of termination is an index of reduced therapeutic potential.

Implicit values influence therapeutic potential

The same content may be communicated in many different ways. The way that is chosen manifests and communicates a particular participant's understanding of the nature of the relationship. For example, "Hello" and "How do you do" are both greetings. "Hello" suggests closeness and a lack of formality and rules. "How do you do" comunicates distance and formality. Even the same word can express different structures of a relationship. "Hello" may communicate "Come on in, I have been expecting you. We have work to do," or it may communicate "Oh, here is the pest again; why do you keep bothering me?"

It is a simple assumption that the way the therapist structures the relationship is a major determinant of therapeutic potential. The therapist's structure can only be expressed in terms of a number of beliefs and values. The problem for the therapist is to conform all of his actions to the structure that can best support the therapeutic processes of substituting and contrasting. The following list of beliefs and values—twelve in number—describes the therapist's structure, as the author conceives of it.

It is not a matter of the therapist taking time out from the therapeutic activity now and then to communicate explicitly his structure of the relationship, but rather it is a matter of his every action conforming to the total therapeutic structure, whether the action has to do with the weather or the client's sexual feelings or an explanation of the therapist's fees. If all actions of the therapist conform to these twelve values a growing therapeutic potential is stored up in the relationship which can be turned into an actual gain by substituting and contrasting. Making the values explicit is irrelevant to therapeutic potential. The values may be made explicit in the interest of working through the content areas described above or in carrying out the process of contrasting. Making them explicit merely draws on the therapeutic potential that is already there but adds nothing to that potential.

1) *The therapist aims at promoting the client's growth and has no other purpose.* The purposes for which ordinary social relationships are formed inevitably complicate and interfere with the use of these relationships for therapeutic purpose. In a business relationship, for example, the aim is to produce some product or render a service. The client's failure to contribute to productivity threatens the stability and continuity of the social organization. In a marital relationship the lives and fortunes of the two people are so interwoven that misfortune of one is a threat to the security of the other parner. If the husband tells his wife that he believes he is having a nervous breakdown, she could hardly help worrying about how the family would manage financially. She could not be expected to say, as a therapist might: "What makes you think that?" Her emotional upheaval is understandable but it probably does not contribute to the husband's growth. Communications from the client about his fears for his mental stability are calmly received by the therapist because they contribute to fulfillment of the purpose for which the relationship was established.

The therapist does not aim at direct satisfaction of the social and psychological needs of the client. He aims instead at teaching him how to manage his relationships in the community in a way to gain these satisfactions. If the client becomes intent upon gaining approval and affection from the therapist, the question is raised of why these needs are not satisfied in his relationships in the community. The therapist is not a substitute; he will not make up to the client for what the community withholds from him. He will help the client understand why the community withholds satisfaction and will help the client learn to get what he needs from the community. Because he is gaining partial satisfaction from his community relationships, the client is often afraid to change lest he be totally rejected and abandoned. If and to the extent that the therapist acts as a substitute satisfaction, he exposes the therapeutic relationship to this fear of change. He makes the client dependent on him and increases his resistance to changing the nature of the relationship. The major exception to this principle exists for clients at the lower end of the developmental scale. To these clients, the therapist may need to give direct satisfaction, but he must give careful attention to using the relationship he establishes to broaden the client's social life and his fulfillment in other relationships. He must structure the satisfaction he provides as demonstrations, and express his unwillingness to go on indefinitely providing these satisfactions. The therapeutic process of substituting is not generally an exception to the principle; the "substituting" consists in providing new information to alter the client's concepts, not in providing gratification. The fact that the therapist is not using the relationship for the satisfaction of his own social needs tends to remove him from the suspicion of having ulterior motives for evaluating what kind of person the client is. It permits the therapist to point out that it makes no difference to him if the client is dominating; the therapist can certainly tolerate this for the amout of time he will be with the client. Rather, the question is: How does this feature of the client's emotional life influence his relationships with people? In this objective, non-judgmental way, the therapist is able to have the client recognize certain features that society evaluates as bad. The therapist is not saying, "You are dominating and you must stop this." He is asking, "You are dominating, and how does this influence the way people treat you?"

If an ordinary social relationship takes on the purpose of therapy, the course of the interaction is likely to show sudden shifts in orientation. There will be periods of patience and understanding, but these will be disrupted by demands for immediate action to meet the requirements of the non-therapeutic purposes. For example, the time comes when the business will suffer too great a loss to permit further patience with the employee's immaturity. The time comes when the wife's frustrated need for support from her husband overcomes her own patience with her husband. The fact that the therapist has no function other than therapy prevents such abrupt discontinuities in the course of the interaction.

2) *The therapist is interested in the total person.* A person shows different parts of himself in each of his relationships. The same person is a son, a student, a neighbor, a customer, a citizen and so on. As he moves from one relationship to another, his behavior changes. None of the relationships is broad enough to include the total person. For a young man, it may be a relatively simple undertaking to learn to behave like a mature student; yet he can still express his immaturity as son, neighbor, friend, husband and citizen. Apparent improvement in any one of these many relationships may merely be a change in the relationship and not in the total person.

The fact that therapy is concerned with the total person gives to the therapist the freedom to inquire into any aspect of the client's life or any of his relationships. No person in any one of his ordinary social relationships has such freedom. A wife may cause offense by inquiring about her husband's relationships with friends and parents, or about details of his business relationships. In therapy, the client may feel offended by the therapist's inquiries, but the therapist can point out the legitimacy of his inquiry in terms of the basic purpose of the relationship. The client's behavior is self-defeating; he is not permitting the therapist to do the job that he engaged him to do.

3) *The therapist is willing to continue the relationship as long as the client needs and can use it.* In all social relationships there is a real and legitimate need to suppress some feelings and ideas in order to perpetuate the relationship. One does not tell his friend everything, for fear of destroying the friendship. The relatively indestructible quality of the therapeutic relationship offers the client the freedom he needs to become acquainted with him-

self as a total person. Many clients will test this aspect of the relationship in the first interview. The general message is, "I am a bad, weak, ineffective person and I have been this way for many years. Are you sure that you want to try to help me?" The anguish that the client has experienced when people discontinued their relationship with him has made him unwilling to enter any relationship unless he is assured that he will not be hurt by rejection. Only the therapeutic relationship has the structure to absorb such demands. By his total manner, not just by what he says, the therapist must communicate his willingness to form and maintain a relationship to the client. The high stability increases the therapist's freedom of action as well as that of the client. Committing himself to such loyalty to the client is necessary in order to take the freedom to raise upsetting questions.

4) *The therapist aims at knowing the client as he really is.* In any relationship the participants either have a model of what the people should be like in that relationship or they are in the process of developing one. The model tends to constrict the kinds of interactions that take place within the relationship. The client will inevitably bring his models from other relationships into the therapeutic relationship. Since the therapist has not participated in the building of these models, he is at liberty to raise inquiries about how they came into the relationship. He may ask the client why he is always frivolous, why he places so much importance upon being bright and witty, why he believes the therapist is forbidding him to have any fun and so on. The therapist structures a relationship in which the client has no need for distortion of the self. The therapist avoids suggestion, either verbal or non-verbal, of any expectations about what kind of person the client should be. He avoids embarrassing the client in any way about any feature of his emotional life that he reveals. In this way, the therapist communicates to the client that he need not disguise himself and that he can be accepted just as he is. This does not mean that the therapist approves of the client or that he intends to suggest that the client should remain as he is. It means that the therapist accepts the client as a person who has problems, and that he will take the client as he is as a point of departure. In thus defining the relationship, the therapist aids the client in the process of self-dis-

closure, in the broadening of his awareness of self, and in reducing his tendency to deceive himself about himself. He increases the client's ability to evaluate himself honestly. He enables the client to discover that his deep fears about revealing some aspects of himself are unrealistic in his present life situation.

5) *The therapist is an expert.* At no time should the therapist deny or minimize his expertness. He should not attempt to put the client at ease by "being one of the boys." The expertness of the therapist is too useful and makes too great a contribution to the therapeutic potential to ever be laid aside. The expertness of the therapist tends to increase the client's self-respect; a person of importance and worth and knowledge is interested in him. When the client reveals aspects of himself that are associated with intense anxiety, the therapist's calm manner tends to be reassuring; his expertness enhances this reassurance. If the client respects the expertness of the therapist, he concludes that the problem is not as dangerous as he thought. If he lacks respect for the expertness of the therapist, he merely concludes that the therapist does not understand the nature of the problem. The expertness of the therapist tends to increase the client's freedom and spontaneity. The client is willing to take greater risks, which is essential to the goal of changing his behavior. If the therapist defines himself as an equal of the client, he makes it impossible to provide the client with experiences that will alter his immature attitudes toward authority. The special significance of the therapist's expertness to the success of the identification interactions is discussed in Chapter IX.

6) *The therapist believes that the client needs and can use his help.* At no time should the therapist disguise or distort the basic purpose of the relationship. Even if the client takes offense at the idea that the therapist believes him to be in need of help, the therapist must quietly assert this evaluation. The therapist need not argue or defend his evaluation but he must maintain it. To disregard this reality of the relationship tends to open the door to all kinds of distortions of substituting; such interactions with the client, in which he is merely acting out his difficulties in interpersonal relationships, have no corrective value. The client may, for example, undertake to engage the therapist in theoretical dis-

cussions about therapy. He wishes in this way to define the relationship as that between colleagues. The proper response of the therapist is not to carry on such a discussion with the client, but to raise the question of why he finds the acceptance of professional help so embarrassing that he must distort the purpose of his meeting with the therapist.

7) *The therapist aims at an effective relationship, not a safe, pleasant, sociable one.* It is understandable that the client should dread and avoid getting into matters that are associated with unpleasant emotions. The therapist, responsible for promoting the client's growth, cannot take comfort in the pleasantness of the relationship. If the client's life is as pleasant and satisfactory as he is presenting it in therapy, why then, the therapist must ask, does the client consult him.

Some therapists talk of their intention to form a relationship with the client first and then, when this is accomplished, to take up the matter of therapy. Such an approach is likely to result in a relationship that is without therapeutic potential. While it is true that the client's comfort and satisfaction and effectiveness in living is the ultimate goal of the therapy, this ultimate goal can only be reached by some sacrifice of the client's immediate comfort. It is difficult for the client to face up to the unpleasant realities of his life even when the therapist shows no tendency to avoid unpleasantness; it is impossible for the client when the therapist shows great distress at the mention of trouble. The therapist must indicate that he is ready to face this unpleasantness as soon as the client is. If the client must delay, all right, but he must not delay out of consideration for the therapist's comfort. Therapist and client have come together to do a job; the therapist is ready to get on with it.

8) *The therapist believes in the client's potential for growth.* One of the fundamental differences among therapists is in the degree of confidence shown in the client's ability to face and learn to solve his difficulties. Some therapists imply that it is mostly up to them to rescue their clients. Other therapists miss no opportunity in telling a client that it is up to him to get himself out of his unsatisfactory situation. Showing too little confidence in the client robs him of his self-confidence and makes him dependent upon

the judgment of the therapist. Emphasizing too much (and too soon) that the client must do everything himself crushes him with too much responsibility and makes him fearful of it. The therapist can show his confidence without emphasizing the client's responsibility. He can offer his help without taking over the total job. He can complement the client's efforts. The therapist must never be too far ahead of the client. If he is, this may increase the client's confidence in his therapist, but not the client's self-confidence. The client will learn to trust himself to the degree that the therapist trusts him.

9) *The therapist places a high value on the client's awareness of how the client is structuring the relationship.* The attitude of the therapist is: "You are free to do as you like, but I'm being paid to let you know what you are doing. You have a right to know." It is not the intention of the therapist to convey to the client that he should or should not structure the relationship in a particular way. The therapist aims at making all of the facts available to the client that will enable him to make his own decisions. The therapist makes the client aware of the lack of complete agreement between the way he structures the relationship and the way the therapist does. For example, the therapist may point out that the client is asking for decisions about what is good or bad for him, and he may contrast this with the therapist's objective viewpoint. Doesn't it make the client feel uneasy to give to another person such power over him? How did other people react when the client asked them to decide what he should do? In this way, the therapist makes the client aware of expectations that he brings into his interpersonal relationships and how these expectations affect the course of those relationships.

10) *The therapist places a high value on freedom of thought in preparation for action.* The therapist recognizes that what the client does will affect the way other people treat him, which will affect the client's response to other people, and so on. Action toward other people must therefore be shaped and modified and restrained in order to establish and maintain interpersonal relationships. The client needs to be very free in thinking about himself, his feeling, his goals and his problems in getting along with other people. If he feels angry with his boss, he needs to be able

to recognize that feeling openly and without disguise. It may be very unwise for him to express his feeling in action toward his boss. It is not necessary to express in action everything that he feels and thinks. The freedom to think brings with it vast new possibilities for actions appropriate to the problem.

11) *The therapist believes there is a rational explanation for the client's behavior.* The therapist's belief that there is a reason for what the client does and feels encourages the client's search for a better understanding of himself. The client usually feels that he is different from people or that some part of his behavior is out of his control. The therapist's belief is reassuring. The client's hope of understanding his behavior and exercising greater control over it provides a motivation of the client for therapy which the therapist can fully share.

12) *The therapist has a deep respect for the dignity and worth of the client.* In ordinary social relationships the thoughts and feelings and motives of an individual are never laid quite so bare as they are in therapy. Such exposure is necessary to the therapeutic purpose. It is unthinkable that it could ever take place unless the therapist respected the client. It is also unthinkable that there would be anything therapeutic about such an exposure if it brought contempt to the client. The fact that the therapist has such a relatively complete view of the client and still can and does respect him is deeply reassuring to the client and tends to enhance his self-respect. The therapist's respect for the client is thus necessary, not only to insure that the client will interact with increasing honesty but also to insure that, as he does, it relieves his fear of rejection through exposure.

Discussion and references

Each action between therapist and client influences their relationship, making it more suitable or less suitable to fulfill its therapeutic purpose; yet this influence is generaly ignored in the literature. Usually the therapist describes either what he does or what he conceives to be necessary to do so that therapy can take place. From here the focus shifts entirely to the carrying out of the therapy. No attention is given to how the specific way in which therapist and client interact affects the relationship. Chances in the client, usually theoretical changes, are noted, but not changes in the relationship. Such a view is a consequence of regarding the method or technique of therapy as a constant, as do classical analysts (Muroe, 1955), behavior therapists (Eysenck, 1960) and client-centered therapists (Rogers, 1961). But if it is believed that method and technique are an inflection of the kind of disorder, then a constant vigilance must be maintained to insure the suitability of the relationship for its therapeutic purpose. The Neo-Freudians have generally undertaken to shape the relationship so that it meets the specific requirements of the patient, but they do not propose (nor, to the author's knowledge, do others) what seems obvious: that all actions between therapist and client influence the suitability of the relationship for carrying out the therapeutic program. Surely no one would oppose the idea that relationships, conceived in all their infinite variety, are differentially suited to a given therapeutic purpose. Presumably, Freud would conceive of the suitability in terms of the client's willingness to lie on the couch and follow the basic rule of free association—a definite role for the patient—and the therapist maintaining a neutral attitude and offering interpretations to the patient—a definite role for the analyst. Rogers would conceive of it in terms of specified attitudes of the therapist—a definite role. The behavior modifiers would conceive of it in terms of the therapist's carefully following the requirements of his learning theory model—a definite role for the therapist. The systems handle the problem of suitability by taking specific actions (structuring) to insure compliance of therapist and patient with the models of role. All systems thus have an unfortunate resemblance to the social structure of schizophrenic families as described by Wynne (1958). In contrast, the author's system would require the therapist to maintain a continuing vigilance which would be directed at every action, not selected classes of actions, between therapist and client. Structuring continues throughout the course of therapy; it is not limited to its beginning. Action of both therapist and client is changing; neither has a fixed role.

The system conceives of a controlled and carefully supervised relationship. On this point, the author has strong allies in Rosen

(1964) and Krasner (1966). Rosen insists that the therapeutic relationship is deliberately aimed at relief, for the benefit of the patient not the therapist; to be therapeutic, it must be controlled and guided all the way. Krasner notes that behavioristic therapy is a deliberate modification of behavior and that the therapist manipulates and controls the situation to attain a specific objective. He emphasizes that therapists must accept a level of responsibility to correspond with planned influence.

This chapter has presented a model for determining priority for the therapist's actions, and has discussed the order in which the client's behavior will be modified. Ford and Urban (1963) note the lack of any logical basis for deciding priority in the systems they review. The development of this aspect of the author's system would provide the basis for focused or limited therapy. It would enable the therapist to provide partial help when practical conditions do not permit setting the goal of bringing the client to full maturity.

The terms used in this chapter, such as bias of communication and dominating motive of the client, may give the impression that the author has left the objectivity and empiricism of the last chapter. This is not the case. The concepts do not have the status of intervening variables (Tolman, 1951) but are purely descriptive, summarizing representations of actions. The observations summarized under the concept of bias of communication are those showing a consistency of client response to a broad range of therapist actions. It is a persistent inappropriateness of response. A dominating motive of the client is a persistent direction of the client's action that is not in accord with the therapeutic objective. It is purely descriptive of what is observed. Perhaps instead of dominating motive, it could have been called persistent misdirection of action.

Finally the author's system offers a model of multiple function of all action. It is as if client and therapist were interacting in a room surrounded by many trick mirrors. The therapist must see the shape of the action as it is reflected by all of these many mirrors. He must register the implication of every action for the beliefs listed and, as the next chapter will show, for the many technical requirements of carrying out the therapeutic program.

While all the many reflections of the actions can be summarized
in terms of increasing therapeutic potential and producing therapeutic gain, such orderliness is not readily apparent in the therapy
room.

Achieving Therapeutic Gain

For the purpose of pursuing therapeutic gain, the client's action in the session may be understood in terms of whether it aims at structuring the relationship in a way 1) that will permit expression and fulfillment at his emotional level or 2) that has no emotional significance. As a matter of narrative convenience, these two kinds of client actions will be referred to as approach and avoidance, respectively. The client's emotional needs push him toward approach behavior; his painful experiences in the past—failure, disillusionment, humiliation—move him toward avoiding any effort to find emotional fulfillment in relationships with other people. The therapist's actions that respond to the client's avoidance behavior culminate in *preparatory* therapeutic gain; the actions that are directed toward the client's approach behavior culminate in *fulfilling* therapeutic gain.

The therapist will give priority to the modification of avoidance behavior not only because of its implications for therapeutic potential but also because the client's growth depends upon a progressively more honest and direct expression of emotional needs. The beginning phase of therapy is dominated by the client's avoidance behavior. Not until the middle phase is reached does the client's action show a major emphasis of approach behavior, and only then can the therapist's actions be directed primarily at modification of the client's emotional level. The changes of the client's behavior in the middle and terminal phases should approximate the normal developmental process.

The achievement of therapeutic gain depends upon the proper application of the therapeutic processes, substituting and contrasting. Both therapeutic processes are applicable to avoidance and

81

approach behavior, and at all levels of the developmental scale. Since the role of the therapist in these two processes and his preparation of the therapeutic relationship are quite different and in some ways contradictory, it is necessary to decide whether the therapeutic program will be 1) one that primarily emphasizes substituting and that uses contrasting merely to support the substituting or 2) whether the emphasis will be on contrasting, with substituting limited to a supporting role. These two kinds of therapeutic programs and the author's ideas about the applicability and technical management of them are presented below.

Planning the substituting

The construct of substituting is abstract. It refers to the relationship between inferable properties of the therapist's action and those of actions that others took toward the client in his development. To qualify as substituting, the therapist's action must have a meaning that is different from that which the client has experienced in the past, and there must be a rational basis to assume that the therapist's action will make up for some deficit in the client's experience, and that this substituting will permit the client to grow. The construct is built on observations of the actions of the therapist, which must be interpreted in terms of their symbolic meaning. For example, the therapist's program for substituting may require that he communicate acceptance of the client. The acceptance is never directly observable. What is observable are all sorts of actions of the therapist which must be interpreted in terms of the degree of acceptance of the client that they communicate. In addition, the construct requires that the therapist hypothesize about what kind of developmental history the client has had and what sorts of experiences he has either missed or had in a distorted form, so that he was prevented from going through the normal developmental process.

The control of substituting as a therapeutic process in the moment-to-moment interaction is even more complicated. Since the therapist is concerned with many matters, he is never able to give his full attention to the process of substituting. Because the process is complex, the therapist should have clearly in mind his program of substituting—the specific kind of experiences which he intends, through his actions, to communicate to the client.

In addition, the program of substituting is helpful to the therapist because it permits a periodic evaluation of the concurrence between the program and his actions up to a particular time. The program of substituting will come from three sources: 1) his understanding of the general nature of developmental deviations, 2) the specific developmental deviation of the particular client, and 3) the therapist's interpretation of the moment-to-moment interaction.

One feature common in developmental deviations is an exposure to degradation, sometimes subtle and sometimes open, but degradation no matter. Consequently the therapist will include in his program of substituting the message: "You are a person of dignity and worth; I regard you as such." The therapist will communicate this message by his every action. To some extent it is a matter of judgment whether an action is in accord with this message or not, but there are guides for that judgment. The client's response to the therapist's action is one source of information about what message the therapist's action conveys. In his experiences with many clients, the therapist will learn which actions make the client feel important and worthwhile and which actions have a reverse effect. Another way in which the therapist may improve his judgment is to practice considering alternative actions as possibilities for the achievement of a particular end. The difference is vast betwen the therapist who, when he runs out of other tasks, has an aide yell across the room that the client is now to come to see the therapist and the therapist who asks the patient what hour would be agreeable with him for their session. The former action may be superior for the convenience of the therapist. The latter is far superior in communicating to the client his worth, value and dignity as a person; it implies that the therapist understands that the client has other commitments and pursuits, and that the therapist would not wish to interfere with these other interests. It implies that the client's time and effort are worth something. It establishes that the therapist does not expect the client to act solely in accord with the therapist's convenience. It establishes a beginning in the movement toward mutuality. The therapist communicates that the client must respect the fact that the therapist has other commitments, and in return the therapist will respect the same fact in regard to the client. As another example, compare the implication of having the client sit down in essentially the same way as the therapist with that of having the client lie down and the therapist sit up and out of sight. The difference in implication is not as blatant as in the previous example and is perhaps more subject to a difference of judgment. If a client understands that the difference in posture between him and the therapist is a technical requirement of a psychological process, the implication about his dignity may be softened. Nevertheless, in the author's opinion, having the client lie while the therapist sits tends to communicate that the therapist makes a fundamental difference of status that is permanent and unalterable. Never will the therapist lie down; never will the client sit back of him. The difference of posture tends to establish a closed, stratified society. It is impossible for the author to imagine that interactions taking place with the client lying and the therapist sitting would ever approach mutuality.

Another common feature in developmental deviations is an excess of experiences in which the client was the participant of lesser power. Then, when the client comes to the therapist for help, he conventionally accepts a lower status. In addition, all developmental deviations result in a failure to progress to emotional maturity and, thus, in a continuing preference for lower status. All of these considerations favor a dependent relationship. The therapist's task is to manage the dependency so that his actions neither block the client's gradual approach to adult status nor push the client into a role and status for which he is not prepared. Perhaps the best way this item of the program of substituting may be worded is: "You are in the process of becoming my equal and independent of me." Such a message permits the client to cling to the therapist as much as his emotional level requires him to do but it also leaves him free to move toward independence as rapidly as his fears will permit.

Perhaps the major source of the program of substituting is the therapist's theory of developmental deviation. The author believes that the decisive difference between the psychotic deviation and normal development is the difference in the kind and degree of support that the mother gives to the child's efforts to relate himself to other people. Thus the major and dominating consideration, the strategy of therapy for the psychotic deviation, is that the therapist's action could substitute for the experiential deprivation. The essential message of the therapist's action is: I am here if you need me, but there are a lot of people in this world who are interesting and worthwhile and whom you would enjoy knowing and with whom you might do things together in satisfying your own needs. The communication of this message requires that the therapist be careful in response to the client's flattery, his talk of experiences with other authorities and his severe rejection of peers. The therapist's action must not convey that he gains any pleasure from the client's forsaking all others for him alone. Nor must it communicate that the therapist believes he is all-sufficient for the client.

Finally, the program of substituting must include an implicit action reply to the implicit question of the client's action, a reply that has substitutive value. Some examples of this kind of substituting are presented in the section "Tests of the Therapist and How He Passes." The two previous sources of the program of substituting set up requirements for the therapist's action that continue throughout the course of the therapeutic program. The moment-to-moment communication with the client sets up requirements for the therapist's action that are current and critical, but temporary and transient. This kind of interaction between therapist and client, this kind of substituting can best be described in terms of the implicit question raised by the client's action and the therapist's implicit reply. It must be kept in mind that the exchange is made through total actions of therapist and client that seldom and epiphenomenally culminate in an actual verbal question and a verbal reply. Some of the questions and answers of this kind in the course of therapy with the psychotic deviation are the following.

Q.   You do not care anything about me, do you?

A.   Yes I do.

Q.   I am too badly off for you to help me, am I not?

A.   I believe you can be helped. I would like to give it further consideration.

Q.   You are going to reject me and hurt me like everyone else, aren't you?

A.   I am willing to continue working with you within the limitations on which we agreed as long as you need me.

Q.   You will only like me if I think well of you alone, isn't that true?

A.   I think there are a lot of good people in the world and and I have no special need for nor pleasure in such absolute loyalty to me.

The therapist replies by action, and he must do it in such a manner that his substitution assists and encourages the client in actions that raise and communicate in many different ways the same question. The client raises the question expecting one answer and receives from the therapist another. This is a reconditioning of the client, an alteration of his ideas about what other people think and expect of him.

Arrangements for the program of substituting

The broad professional training and clinical experience of the therapist, which would have to be considered in any comprehensive coverage of the matter of arrangements, is assumed. Apart from this, the additional arrangements for carrying out the program of substituting may be broken down into arrangements, relating to the organizational obligations of the therapist and those relating to actual shaping of the relationship with the client.

A few illustrations will clarify the meaning of the phrase "the organizational obligations of the therapist." Consider the therapist who works in an organization committed to custody. Membership in such an organization means that the adequacy of the therapist's work, the esteem in which he is held, and his social rewards in the organization depend upon the degree to which his actions contribute to custody. The program of substituting, however, conflicts with the actions that would be required to insure best that the client does not injure himself or other people. The therapist's position in the custodial organization is jeopardized if he remains committed to the program of substituting. It is absurd to assume that the therapist could carry out the program of substituting in such a situation, regardless of the excellence of his training or knowledge. Consider another illustration, perhaps a more current one. The therapist functions in an organization that is committed to giving first-aid, emergency assistance to the client and quickly sending him on his way. The objective of the organization is to keep the turnover at the proper statistical level. The therapist is valued if he dismisses the clients quickly. If he delays the departure of the clients for whom he is responsible, he is shown the appalling statistics. The program of substituting requires that the therapist not block the client's progress toward independence and toward leaving treatment, but it also requires that he not pressure the client into acting out an emotional maturity that is fictitious. The therapist cannot ignore these kinds of organizational influences on his practice of therapy.

It violates every insight into the forces that control behavior to assume that mere knowledge of his program will enable the therapist to carry it out. Yet the professional literature, with rare exceptions, reflects such an assumption. Relatively little attention has been given to the social conditions in which the therapist does his work. There appears to be a rather general assumption that knowing about the client and his pecularities and about how to do therapy is all that is needed to carry on therapy. As regards the client, no such assumption is made. He is subject to the social conditions that surround him and he behaves in accordance with pressures from these social conditions, even when he knows it is not the wise thing to do. Obviously, the therapist must accept responsibility for judging and arranging the social conditions for therapy so that they will support him in carrying out his work. If the therapist does not, then no one can or will.

The therapist then is obligated to make clear to the organization what the necessary arrangements are for the practice of therapy. If he cannot achieve the necessary organizational support for his practice, he should, in the author's opinion, refuse to do therapy or, more exactly, to pretend doing it. To proceed with "therapy" under organizational conditions that block all hope of success is as serious a breach of propriety as for a surgeon to proceed with an operation under septic conditions.

On the other hand, the therapist cannot expect to work in organizational conditions that are perfect. It is for him to determine the point at which conditions are so inadequate as to leave little hope of success. The therapist is responsible for making such a judgment and for acting in accord with his judgment or for asking for consultation.

The basic objectives of the professional organizations to which the therapist belongs may be expected to exert a similar, but less intense, influence over his ability to carry out his program. The question is: How serious is the commitment of the profession to the objective of therapy, the growth of every person to his full adult stature and effectiveness? Clearly this goal is different from that of direct relief of suffering of either social or psychological origin. It is also distinguishable from the scientific objective to develop a system of principles of empirical validity that describe behavioral phenomena.

The compensation of the therapist for his work, whether it is from an organization or directly from the client, can be incorporated in this conceptual framework. The program of substituting requires actions of accepting the client. Can the therapist be relied upon to take such actions if he is inadequately rewarded for his service to the client?

Another source of limitation is the community. The therapist is a member of the community and must be responsive to the goals of that organization. If the community demands increased protection from the therapist's clients, the organizations to which it has delegated the responsibility must respond by increased emphasis on custody. Ultimately it is the community that decides these matters. If the therapist is to do his job, he must make his objectives clear to the community and receive its endorsement and support. He need not merely abide by the community's judgment; he can influence and shape it.

In summary, the therapist can most effectively carry out the program of substituting when in doing so he fulfills his obligations to the organization in which he works and to the profession and community of which he is a part. The therapist needs to understand that in shaping his obligations in these social organizations he is making arrangements that are necessary for therapy.

The other aspect of making the necessary arrangements, that of shaping the relationship of the client, has received much more attention in the professional literature. Almost every treatment of the subject of therapy includes a section on the limitation of the relationship. What is not generally recognized is that the content of these limitations should be determined by what is necessary to support the program of substituting. Using acceptance of the client to illustrate the point: Can the therapist communicate acceptance of the client if he permits the client to wake him repeatedly in the early hours of the morning, to interrupt his dinner with his family, to call him for the flimsiest of reasons, and so on. No, he cannot, and the normality of the therapist if he attempted to do so would be highly suspect; he would structure a relationship in which the client would not be prevented from abusing the therapist, which could only increase the client's burden of guilt and difficulty in maintaining self-respect.

The therapist must set the limits that are necessary to carry out the program of substituting. He must protect values that are essential to the therapeutic process. Placing limitations on the demands that the client can make of the therapist may appear to be reducing the client's liberty. Actually the limitations are essential to establish it. The limitations establish boundaries within which the client is free to do as he pleases, just as the backyard fence frees the toddler of the mother's constant interruption of his play in the interest of safety. With the appropriate limitations the therapist can communicate a degree of acceptance of the client not otherwise obtainable.

By establishing limitations the therapist can shape the relationship so that it becomes suitable for its specific therapeutic purpose. The chapter "Shaping the Therapeutic Contact" presents the author's specific solution of this general therapeutic problem in the case of the psychotic deviation.

Doing the substituting

Even with carefully laid plans and suitable arrangements the actual substituting is still complex. There is not enough empirical description of the process of substituting over the course of therapy, as it moves through the developmental scale, to delineate the route clearly. The therapist must still rely heavily on his carefully acquired skill in interpreting the relationship and in expressing messages about the relationship in his actions. What can be done here is to show the general nature of the problem and indicate the form of assistance that empirical observation of the process and careful description could give.

Those values in the program of substituting that are derived from the general nature of developmental deviations and from the theory of the particular kind of developmental deviation of the client remain constant throughout the course of therapy. The therapist will express his acceptance of the client and his respect for his dignity from beginning to end. The mode of expressing these values, however, must change as therapy produces movement of the client along the developmental scale. The way one expresses acceptance of an infant is vastly different from the way one expresses acceptance of a child. To the infant, it is expressed in vigorous actions of smiling, laughing, making faces, goo-gooing and physical contact. The same kind of actions toward the child would not be acceptance but an offense to his dignity. He would feel that he was being treated like a baby and thus insulted. Empirical research could do much to assist the therapist in that it could carefully describe how the various essential values are expressed by the therapist at each level of the developmental scale.

On the other hand, the question the client raises by his action about the nature of the relationship is constantly changing, and thus the answer made by the therapist must change. The problem here is not the expression of constant values in ever changing form, but how to interpret the question the client raises and how to make a reply that will resolve his question. The author assumes that when substituting is applied to clients of the same kind of developmental deviation, there is a movement through the same series and order of questions and answers. Not only this but these questions and answers must be expressed in the same kind of ways. It is clearly an empirical problem then as to what the order of these questions and answers is and how they are expressed.

Finally, the author looks forward to the day when the therapist will be assisted by objectively derived indices of whether the substituting is on or off course. Such indices would direct the therapist in making the necessary adjustments in his actions to insure repeatable results in the same way as the indices of pressure and temperature direct the industrial engineer. The indices would not document the basic nature of the process; they would merely signal the need for adjustive actions from the therapist. These indices would not and could not replace the judgment of the therapist, but they would assist and give increased accuracy to judgments that must now be made by skillful interpretation of the interpersonal interactions.

Contrasting in the service of substituting

A therapeutic program emphasizing substituting means that the therapist's fundamental purpose is to expose the client during the sessions to an interpersonal world that is fundamentally different from that of the client's developmental deviation. To assist the client in a verbalization of the contrast is a secondary objective and is attended to only to the extent that it furthers the primary one. During an emphasis of substituting, the psychological force that stimulates therapeutic gain is the impact of the therapist's actions on the client, which stimulates the client to alter his interpretation of the identity of himself and other people. The need for contrasting as a supporting process arises out of the fact that the client may interpret the therapist's actions in ways that destroy their therapeutic power. It thus becomes essential for the effectiveness of substituting that the process of contrasting be used to alter the client's interpretation of the therapist's actions. For example, the client may consider the interpersonal world displayed in the therapy sessions as an isolated one without implications for the real social world. The therapist treats him the way he does because he is the therapist and he is supposed to treat clients that way. Such an interpretation defeats the therapist's objective which is to demonstrate to the client that it is possible for him to change the form of his relationships to people, that relationships to people need not have the destructive and morbid qualities which his have had in the past. Substituting is powerless to alter this interpretation of the client. The interpretation must be made a verbal issue, which is the essence of contrasting.

To give another and different kind of example; the client may interpret the actions of the therapist aimed at protecting values essential to the therapeutic process as evidence of the therapist's intention to dominate him. His experiences with people have taught him to expect domination; he is unable to distinguish between domination and the exercise of reasonable authority. The making of an intra-class distinction, such as domination versus reasonable authority, is a problem to be solved by contrasting.

Contrasting in the service of substituting seldom goes beyond the question of how the client is structuring the relationship to the therapist. Even this initial question is handled in a more casual and incidental way than it would be in a therapeutic program that emphasizes contrasting. Another distinction is that the therapist does not make a verbal issue of all of the ways in which the client is distorting the relationship but only of those that have critical importance to the effectiveness of substituting. The importance of contrasting to the attainment of the therapeutic objectives becomes progressively greater with movement along the developmental scale. The point on that scale at which the therapeutic program of substituting and contrasting in the service of substituting shifts to contrasting and substituting in the service of contrasting is best left for further study. The author proposes that the shift should occur in Childhood, not at first but before the end of that stage.

Planning the contrasting

For several reasons the coverage of contrasting in this book will be less complete than that of substituting. For one thing, by far the larger part of the author's therapeutic experience has been at the level of Childhood and below, which means a greater experience with substituting than contrasting. Another consideration is that the professional literature is far more adequate and complete in the description of contrasting than it is in that of substituting. In much of the literature the definition of psychotherapy is identical to that of contrasting and the process of substituting is not recognized. Also the coverage must be brief because an adequate description of so complex a process would fill a book in itself. Contrasting is complex not because of the basic and logical nature of the operation, but because of the great diversity of emotional life on the Childhood and higher levels. Emotional life is much simpler at those levels to which substituting is applied, and therefore the description and technical control of the process is simpler. With movement along the developmental scale, symbolism becomes progressively more abstract, more difficult and more complex, and this increases the complexity of contrasting. The author's belief that careful observation and description of the process of substituting might reveal a relatively stable order of questions and answers and might reveal forms in which these are expressed in interpersonal action has no room in the case of contrasting. The therapist must rely much more on his broad clinical experience to be able to interpret the interpersonal meanings of his client's actions. Finally, the author's major concern is the design of the therapeutic program for the psychotic deviation, and for this purpose contrasting is of relatively little significance.

If the client begins in therapy with a program emphasizing substituting, the first problems encountered by the therapist in the planning of contrasting are those related to when and how to make the shift. Since the role of the therapist, the shaping of the therapeutic contact and the preparation of the relationship differ considerably in these two processes, on theoretical grounds, the transition would be expected to be difficult. On the other hand, in normal development the educators of children who follow their growth over a number of years make a transition from a communication with them that emphasizes interpersonal action to one that emphasizes verbal and symbolic interactions. Since these educators are able to make this transition without the specialized training of the therapist, he should be able to solve the problem of transition adequately. For the time being, the author would prefer to leave this question open. At any event, it may be more practical and more economical with a scarce resource, the therapist's time, to recommend a change of therapists to the client. Such a change would avoid the problem of transition and would permit the new therapist to begin shaping the relationship that could best serve the process of contrasting without having to relate that relationship to the one with the previous therapist.

The essential operation of contrasting is the comparison of actual relationship with the client's structure. Thus the simpler, clearer and more straightforward the actual relationship is, the better. The therapist must make no move that would confuse or complicate the actual relationship. This requirement is clearly in conflict with what is required in substituting. All of the actions required of the therapist in communicating the program of substituting tend to obscure the most simple and, for the purposes of contrasting, most useful actual relationship: The therapist is the paid assistant of the client who will help him overcome some of his developmental limitations.

The dominating consideration of maintaining a simple, straightforward relationship also makes it undesirable for the therapist to have any obligations to the client other than those of therapy. If the therapist is given the obligation for the general supervision of the client in an institution, this responsibility will require the therapist to take actions that are in conflict with the simple, clear, actual relationship that is technically desirable. The acceptance of custodial responsibility would result in even more serious conflict. For example, if the client complains of abuse from the institutional personnel, the therapist with only therapeutic responsibility undertakes to understand himself, and to assist the client in understanding, the meaning of this communication for the relationship between client and therapist. Is the client accusing the therapist of not taking good care of him or is he praising the therapist for being the only one who does not abuse him? The action of the client may have any one of thousands of such interpersonal meanings. If the therapist has custodial responsibility, he is required to investigate the reality of what the client is communicating, and is thus taken off course from his therapeutic objective. The actions the therapist takes in his interrogation of the client to assist him in determining whether the client has in fact been abused encourages the client in his beliefs that the therapist has very broad, general, parent-like reponsibility for his welfare. It encourages the client to complain in order to have the therapist take corrective actions rather than accept the therapeutic objective that he, the client, take the corrective actions.

Looking at the other side, the client's structure, there is the technical requirement that the therapist's actions must not block and, if possible, should facilitate the client's actions aimed at structuring the relationship in accordance with his emotional life. Luckily this requirement is in accord with that of a simple, clear, actual relationship. Both objectives are well served if the therapist takes only few and well-measured actions. In order to maintain a clear standard for comparison, the therapist, from time to time, will need to communicate his understanding of the actual relationship. Except for these few measured actions the therapist will leave the structuring of the relationship to the client. He will permit the client to attribute to him whatever role and identity he chooses. Actions of the therapist which communicate his identity as a person tend to structure the relationship and, because of the high status of the therapist, to block the client from structuring the relationship in accordance with his preferences. Thus for the purposes of contrasting, the therapist through his actions will confront the client with a passive and neutral image. He will then proceed to make the client aware of the identity and image that he imposes on the neutral one. The apparent reverse of making the client more aware of the identity he gives himself through his actions is, in fact, but another route to the discovery of the identity he attributes to the therapist. The identities of therapist and client are interlocking like those of student and teacher. The discovery that the client conceives of himself as a person in need of instructions reveals that he conceives of the therapist as both able and responsible for instructing him.

Arranging the contrasting

The principle that the therapist's organizational commitments should not conflict with what is required for the technical management of the process applies to contrasting as much as to substituting. The therapist needs to arrange to have no other responsibility for the client than that of pursuing therapeutic gain. He must insure that practical considerations, like time, money and opportunity for enough sessions to achieve the therapeutic objective, do not preclude the use of contrasting.

Shaping the therapeutic contact to support contrasting is more than establishing limitations; it becomes a matter of absolute avoidance of any subterfuge for carrying on the interaction with the client. The technical requirement of a simple, clear, actual relationship makes it mandatory that the therapist not undertake to do contrasting after being introduced to the client as a friend of the family. Neither can he do contrasting incidentally to an examination of a stubbed toe or the treatment of a bad stomach. Contacts with the client outside of regularly scheduled therapy sessions are undesirable in contrasting, much more so than in substituting. The therapist's careful measurement of every one of his actions to insure a passive, neutral image and a simple, clear, actual relationship is difficult or impossible to maintain without careful limitation of outside contacts. The therapist's planned avoidance of revealing his identity in the therapy session is destroyed if the client interacts with him on social occasions in which the therapist's identity is amply broadcast. Outside contacts tend to blur the actual relationship, making the contrasting more difficult and time consuming, and thus reduce the therapeutic potential of the relationship.

The process of contrasting requires that the client does not demand immediate results; he must be prepared to make an investment that is much like that of a student. For this reason contrasting should not be undertaken when the client's social adjustment is collapsing or when he is under strong social or situational pressure. To undertake contrasting at such a time is somewhat like trying to show a person the advantages of a new house while the one he is living in burns down. First, the fire must be put out; then consideration can be given to other possible living arrangements.

Doing the contrasting

Skillful and successful employment of the process of contrasting to attain therapeutic gain is far more dependent upon the broad experience and training of the therapist in matters of interpersonal relationships than is substituting. The range and diversity of interpersonal messages and the forms in which they are expressed is vastly greater in contrasting than in substituting. The therapist's training will teach him to handle the actual relationship in a standard way; he turns it into a given for the solving of the key problem, that of inferring the client's structure of the relationship.

In logical order, the basic questions of the operation are: How is the client structuring the relationship? Why is he structuring it this way? Would he not find another kind of structure more fulfilling? In practice these questions are never developed according to such a neat scheme. Nevertheless, the three questions provide convenient categories for the therapist in classifying his observations and in making his decisions of what actions he might take to further the process. The question of "how" is one of the picture the client paints of himself and of the therapist, of what feelings and motives he attributes to each, what expectations he has of the therapist, and what he thinks the therapist expects of him. The question of "why" is a further specification of how. "Why" moves the content of the interaction to the developmental history of the client. Why develops the question of how in terms of length of duration and extent of applicability of a behavioral characteristic in the history of the client's interpersonal relationships. Why also raises the question of what emotional problems the structure solves for the client. Does he remain a child because he values the gratifications of childhood or because he is afraid that his aggressive feelings would be completely unmanageable if he assumed adult power? The question of why makes clear what sort of experiences the client needs in order to overcome the block in his development. If the block is a matter of gratification, he must experience adult gratifications. If it is a matter of control of impulses, he must have experiences that will teach him to be less fearful and insecure about his ability to control himself. The question of why other possibilities should be more fulfilling, is the reverse side of the coin. Instead of pointing at the emotional problems that are being solved by the way the client structures the relationship, it becomes now the question of how such a structure limits him and reduces his effectiveness as a person, and how he could make things better for himself.

Every action of the client provides the therapist with the opportunity to infer the structure of the relationship. Skilled therapists differ on the relative importance given to various kinds of actions and the time at which an inference should be offered to the client for consideration. The author has no special solution for the proper timing of verbal interpretations to the client. The best rule he knows is borrowed from obstetrics: When in doubt, wait. There is, however, another and more complicated consideration which can guide the therapist. The client will communicate his message to the therapist in many different ways, initially through gestures and tangential verbalization, then increasingly in a direct and verbal manner. As long as the therapist can witness these changes, he can let nature take its course. When this movement stops, he must raise the question of how he is blocking the client's movement. The client beats around the bush but he hits closer and closer to the bush unless the therapist blocks him. If he stops, the client has discerned that the therapist is threatened by the movement toward the bush. He stops out of consideration for the therapist's security, which is vital to his own. Success of the therapist in using contrasting is more one of not blocking the client than it is of giving assistance to him. If the therapist can bear to hear what the client has to say, the client is so reassured by the therapist's equanimity that he will speak of the ordinarily unmentionable. Whether it is fantasy of destruction or incest, the therapist must be able to listen with the posture of a sphinx, or at least with a poker face.

This movement from a peripheral and gestural to a direct and verbal message is essential to the therapeutic effectiveness of contrasting. It is generally believed among therapists that the speed of this process can be increased by the therapist in that he offers to the client verbal summaries of the interpersonal meaning of the client's action. These verbal summaries are called interpretations. But therapists differ fundamentally about what they interpret to the client and when they do it. Because of the diversity, the author's position on these issues needs to be stated.

The author would interpret the interpersonal meaning of the

client's action, that is, how the client defines himself, the therapist and the relationship between the two; what he expects of each and how he proposes to get what he expects. At no time would the author be interested in showing to the client the bare, naked impulse within himself. There might be some discussion about what impulse the client felt, but this would be preliminary to relating that impulse to the client's structure of the relationship, as "You feel angry because I neglect you." The symptoms of the client, when they become interpretable, would be treated in a similar way. The explanation that the client's paralyzed arm protects him from becoming violently aggressive, while correct, is beside the point, from the author's point of view. The client's paralyzed arm defines him as a person who cannot assume responsibility for control of his impulse and defines the therapist as one who will accept this responsibility for him. It is this definition of the relationship that the author believes is critical and makes the proper content of the interpretation.

On the question of timing, the author prefers that whatever is to be interpreted be clearly visible in the interpersonal interaction, its presence in fantasy or in reports of dreams is too removed. The author would view a report of a dream by the client as tentative test of whether he might bring the kind of relationship depicted in the dream into the one with the therapist. It is a tangential, faint questioning of whether it would be all right or not. The therapist is constant throughout the course of therapy in affirming that he wishes to hear all the client has to say. With this kind of answer to the report of the dream, the client will move toward a more direct and verbal expression.

Substituting in the service of contrasting

The use of substituting in a therapeutic program emphasizing contrasting is limited to the communication of those values that remain constant throughout the therapeutic process, such as acceptance and respect for the client, and to a form of a relationship (within which to do the contrasting) that is basically different from those that characterized the client's developmental deviation. The moment-to-moment communication about matters that are current and critical is pushed up to an entirely verbal level. The therapist does not answer through his actions the questions that the client raises with his. He continues to listen and perhaps to offer interpretations until the question has a verbal form. If he replies in action form, he prevents the question from ever becoming verbalized, which is the objective of contrasting. The essential message of the therapist's actions in response to these moment-to-moment questions is: Tell me more about it; let's talk out rather than act out these messages.

The above requirements for the form of the relationship in which contrasting is carried out have many implications for the choice of technique. At no time should the therapist assume a role of being some sort of wizard who can look into deep and mysterious things, which the client could never hope to do. At no time should the therapist assume a role of his judgment being always best. In fact, the therapist should defer final judgment to the client. He will thus phrase his interpretations as possibilities for the client's consideration. "Are you," "could you be," "it looks like you might be," "it seems like," "do you think" are common phrases of the therapist which help him communicate his program of substituting in the service of contrasting, which is essentially: The therapist is the paid assistant of the client.

Discussion and references

The author's system requires the conclusion that it is a strategic error for the therapist to direct his actions toward the achievement of insight in a program that emphasizes substituting. This is well beyond the defensive position of Dreikurs (1963) that insight is not a prerequisite for cure. Implicit in, and inferable from, the concept of substituting is that the normal developmental sequence is the proper model for therapy. The objective is to present to the client those experiences that in his developmental history have been absent or deviant as compared to those in normal growth. Piaget (Flavell, 1963) has amply documented the movement in normal growth from the particular and concrete to the general and abstract. A program emphasizing insight is totally inappropriate until the person has reached a level of conceptual

development that makes it possible to deal with the abstract. Also
the natural order of growth is to learn first to do things and then
to conceptualize them. The child is able to orient himself in space
with considerable skill before he is able to conceptualize this orientation in either a verbal or pictorial manner. Applying these
empirically documented conclusions about normal conceptual development to the therapeutic problem requires the decision that
before a client can develop insight he must demonstrate in his
behavior a differentiated concept of himself and other people.
Only then can the client move on to the development of a conceptual model of what self is like and what the relation of self to
other person is.

Freud (Munroe, 1955) regarded any "acting out" (communication of interpersonal meanings by behavioral rather than verbal
means) as undesirable, because it prevented verbalization and
thus insight. The author agrees that behavioral and verbal expression are reciprocally related. Also that the general movement in
therapy is, as Ruesch (1955) has proposed, from non-verbal to
verbal expression. Thus the highest level of development and of
therapeutic achievement is represented by the ability to conceptualize the relation of self to other people. The author's difference
is that he insists that this highest level of development cannot be
attained by limiting communication to verbal messages. It can
only be attained by a gradual movement from an emphasis on behavioral expression (substituting) to an emphasis on verbal expression (contrasting). Searles (1965, Chapter 13) agrees with this
view of therapeutic movement.

The author would prefer less emphasis on the distinction between verbal and non-verbal behavior than it has received during
the past era of preoccupation with consciousness and the account-
ing for all of man's inner state of mind. In the phrase of Burrow
(Gault, 1953), the author's concept of action refers to a total
organismic response. This totality may be broken down into categories of verbal and non-verbal, but these should be viewed in
the perspective of the whole. The shift from non-verbal to verbal
expression is merely a change in mode of communication and does
not represent any major reorientation of the organism, as do the
changes from one stage of development to another.

The logical models presented by Loevinger (1966) for analysis of the problems of measurement of ego development are extremely helpful in understanding the therapeutic problems presented in this chapter. Thus, avoidance interaction, preparatory therapeutic gain and polar variables make one set of interlocking terms; approach interaction, therapeutic gain and milestone sequences make another set. Research in psychotherapy in the past has concentrated on the first set; the author believes the second set is more fundamental, and Loevinger points out that milestone sequences are more easily and reliably measured than polar variables.

The idea that the beginning phase of therapy consists of working through the avoidance behavior and eliciting the approach behavior is in general accord with the psychoanalytic development of transference. The author does not, however, regard the approach behavior as in any way specific to the therapeutic situation, nor is it in any special way related to early infantile conflicts that have been dissociated. The approach behavior is a total organismic response which reveals the level of emotional life. Approach interaction is thus stage-specific, but avoidance interaction is not. Since it is stage-specific, it will deal with the crisis problems of Erikson (1963). These problems should, in the author's view, be handled in the same way as in normal development, with the aim of moving the total organism forward rather than merely draining dammed-up infantile emotions. The author believes that the progression in the therapeutic interaction through the avoidance behavior to the approach behavior and forward into an increasingly verbal conceptualization of the crisis problem are the basic data of Freud's intrapsychic dimension of unconscious to conscious.

The presence of invariant values throughout the course of therapy has been emphasized by the non-directive therapists (Rogers, 1961) to the neglect of the changing mode of expression, roughly from non-verbal to verbal, and of the stage-specific crisis problems. Only when the therapeutic program begins to emphasize contrasting does the author's method tend to correspond with non-directive therapy. At the level of contrasting, the author's emphasis on clarity of relationship corresponds to the non-directive insistence on therapist's congruence; the author's non-intervention, except to resolve the block in the flow toward increasingly verbal expression, corresponds to the reliance on self-actualization. The correspondence between methods is only partial, however. As soon as the therapist has an answer to the question of why the client is structuring the relationship in the way he does, the author would urge him to provide experiences (use substituting) to assist the client in overcoming his problem. The non-directive therapist would proceed on a steady course without regard to the assistance that substituting could give. Also, the author would urge a continuing supervision of the contrasting in order to prevent or remedy any distortion of contrasting, which he holds responsible for many therapeutic failures. These considerations make clear that the theoretical difference between the author and non-directive therapy does result in a difference in recommended practice. It is not a mere difference in way of expressing the same thing. Since there is a difference in practice, the theory can be subjected to empirical test.

The therapeutic problem posed by the requirement to express a constant value in continuously changing form is similar to that of an institution, such as the church, that is committed to unalterable values, but which must express these values in constantly changing form in order to be understood in its course through changing social conditions. The author hopes that careful study of this problem in the therapeutic process will assist in the understanding of such sociological and anthropological problems. As regards organizational supports for the therapist, Whitaker et al. (1965) mention the importance of the therapist's security in his professional groups.

This chapter provides further specification of priority and, together with the previous chapter, establishes the schedule of therapist's actions.

The conclusion from the author's theory that the therapeutic process is technically simpler when applied to psychotics than to neurotics may seem to be out of accord with the fact that historically therapy for the neurotic preceded that for the psychotic. According to Tuddenham (1966, p. 216) the branches of mathematics developed historically from most to least difficult. The author believes the same pattern has occurred in the field of therapy.

The author's idea of a dependable, invariant sequence of changes during the therapeutic process has many relatives in the literature, some close and some in appearance only. As an example of the latter, the phases of therapeutic growth discussed by Bach (1954) may be mentioned. Bach's phases are arbitrary divisions of what the author regards as a polar variable (Loevinger, 1966). His phases divide what is a continual flowing change from non-verbal to verbal expression. The content that changes with movement from one developmental stage to another and from one crisis problem to another is either ignored or confused with the changing form of communication. The description of stages by Rogers (1958) is of the same kind. Perhaps what has caused this failure to take account of the milestone sequences is that the change in form of communication characterizes not only the entire course of the therapeutic process but also the course of crisis problems. Piaget has noted a return to egocentrism upon confrontation by a new problem, which quickly disappears at higher levels of development. Thus, Bach's and Roger's conceptualizations of therapeutic phases deal with peripheral not central phenomena. Pious (1961) speaks of a progression of behavioral states, but it is not clear whether he means changing mode of communication or major behavioral reorientation. On the other hand, the description of Bion (1961) of the progressive, orderly changes in a therapeutic group is at least a brother of the author's concept. Bion even describes the communicational biases characteristic of different basic assumptions; this corresponds to the author's idea of interpersonal pattern associated with developmental level. Bion notes that each basic assumption produces its own special frustrations, which corresponds to the author's idea of special problems and dissatisfaction at each stage. Similarly, the stages described by Foulkes and Anthony (1957) are compatible with the author's concept; they too note that members of various developmental levels respond differently to the same communication, that is, they have stage-specific communcational biases.

The orderly sequence of changes in the course of group therapy is the basic observation on which rests the author's theory of the developmental scale: that each stage is a preparation for the next and that each is a fulfillment of the one previous to it. Piaget holds a similar view, but it is based on his observations of children at different stages of development. An agreement in theory arrived at by such different means strongly supports the validity of the theory. The agreement also supports the basic assumption that the therapeutic process is essentially not different from normal growth, from which so much of the author's theory is derived.

The observation of repeatable sequences in the therapeutic process by several therapists has not resulted in the research efforts it deserves. A recent book on research methods (Gottschalk and Auerback, 1966) reports that the technique of making sound motion pictures of therapy sessions is now far advanced. This technique is admirably suited to the study of the therapeutic process as the author conceives of it. It would permit documentation and detailed description of the changing mode of communication and of the pattern of changing questions being asked by clients (stage-specific crisis problems).

Ruesch and Kees (1956) have done much of the groundwork for the empirical study of the changing mode of communication in the therapeutic process. Many of the problems in this area can probably be approached by limited experiments in which the therapist would vary answers to a specific question to determine which is most effective in producing therapeutic gain. The criteria of therapeutic gain are clear: stopping the client from asking the question and moving to a question (stage-specific problem) higher in the sequence. Such studies would both develop and validate therapeutic technique; they may lead to such precision in definition of what the therapist should do to stimulate growth that technicians could be trained to carry out the therapeutic program. This would mean that the social need for therapy and its availability could be more adequately balanced than is the case today.

Shaping the Therapeutic Contact

The grand strategy of psychotherapy for the psychotic deviation is for the therapist to form and progressively improve a parent-like relationship to the client and to use this relationship over an extended period of time to encourage the client to form and maintain relationships with other authority figures and peers. The strategy follows the pattern of the mother in normal development. The therapist is not a parent of the clients and nothing should imply that he is, but like the mother he must make a bridge between his clients and other people. He must provide encouragement and rewards and opportunities for such relationships. In the psychotic deviation the mother has not only failed to provide this essential stimulation for growth but has actively opposed and destroyed the child's efforts to relate himself to other people. It is only in the sense of providing this essential stimulation for growth that the therapist's role is parallel to that of the parent. In other regards it is distinctly different, and the differences must be built into the limitations of the relationship.

How much responsibility should the therapist accept in forming and maintaining the relationship? He must decide this with full consideration of the readiness of the client. If the therapist expects the client to act in a way that is far above his emotional level, he does not establish contact. He structures a relationship that is too far up the developmental scale for the client to understand and participate in it. On the other hand, if he takes too much responsibility, he retards the growth of the client by structuring a relationship too far down the developmental scale to permit the client to use his potential. Ideally, the therapist would be able to structure and participate in a relationship with a client at any point on the developmental scale. In practice, the therapist is likely to be limited and must function within his limitations by selecting clients who need a relationship within the range in which the therapist can effectively participate.

Like the parent of an infant the therapist must take an active role and a great degree of responsibility in creating and maintaining the relationship with psychotic clients. The more infantile the clients are the greater the activity, and the more initiative the therapist must show. In normal development it is the adult who makes funny faces, noises and smiles and so on to attract and focus the attention of the infant upon himself. With very regressed, emotionally very infantile clients the function of the therapist must simulate that of an adult initiating an interaction with a child. He may need to have contact with the clients outside the therapy sessions in order to secure their attendance and cooperation. He cannot wait and insist upon the client reaching out to him; the therapist must reach out to the client. The client should not be asked to choose whether he wishes the relationship with the therapist or not until his emotional development is at a level that would make such a choice meaningful for him. Until the client can share the responsibility for continuing the relationship, the therapist should take full responsibility. The psychotic is usually far along in his treatment before he is able to express a clear, positive commitment of himself to continuing the relationship with the therapist. On the other hand, it is not unusual for a client who says that the relationship means nothing to him and that he is not the least bit interested in it to come regularly to the sessions. The author went through a period of declining to enter in a therapeutic relationship with a client who would not make a choice himself to enter that relationship. In the light of the concept of readiness, this now appears to be no more sensible than the refusal of a parent to take care of an infant unless he says that he wants to be taken care of. It is true that growth proceeds at a faster pace when the client is able to make a choice for the relationship, but growth is faster because he is at a higher level of emotional development, not wholly because of the commitment.

Two strategic problems

By the time a client comes into a therapeutic relationship, he has given up the struggle for a satisfying relationship to another human being, has concluded he is hopelessly different and alien, and has lost himself in his own rambling, vague thoughts about himself and his situation. Years of frustrated, conflictual, stormy, unsuccessful, unproductive and smashingly self-defeating and destructive relationships with people have left their marks. By the time the therapist introduces himself the client has been through hell ten times over. As he sees it, the therapist is but one more of his prosecutors and tormentors.

The emotional life of the client has remained at an infantile level. The only pattern of interpersonal relationship is that which he had with his mother. He frequently shows indifference and apathy, but he may show intense feeling for the therapist for a relatively brief period of time. There can easily be hours and hours of practically no response to the therapist; the client just sits there. On the other hand he may be wildly talkative but with an infantile lack of concern for making himself understood. He is even less concerned about listening to the therapist. His deep contempt for humanity, formed and nourished by the endless frustrations of his interpersonal experience, is expressed in his gross disregard for what others think and feel and judge. He is psychologically deaf to what other people have to say. He has few if any attractive traits; he is not congenial, not stimulating, not witty, not full of interesting ideas, not pleasant, not rewardingly grateful for attention given him. He is contemptuously indifferent. In responding to such a person, reaction is to overlook and reject him. There is one thing about him, however, that to some people has a strong appeal: his excruciating suffering.

The background of the client presents the therapist with two strategic problems in forming and maintaining a therapeutic relationship with him: 1) to limit and minimize the client's contemptuous disregard of others and his consequent use of infantile, unsocialized ways, and 2) to avoid the therapist's rejection of the client. From the very beginning the most serious threat to a successful therapeutic outcome is that the client will provoke the therapist into rejecting him. The author recommends two approaches to these strategic problems: setting the limitations of the relationship and the group mode of contact.

Limitations of the relationship. The essential functions of limitations of the relationship are to insure the security of the therapist and to delineate the professional nature of the relationship. If the client threatens the security of the therapist, rejection naturally follows. The continuity of the relationship thus depends upon limitations that will keep the demands the client may place on the therapist within his tolerance, even if they are continued for an indefinite time. A frequent mistake of the beginning therapist is to disregard the need for limitations in the interest of establishing a relationship with the client. His eagerness leads to an indiscretion that always delays the process of therapy and frequently destroys the therapeutic potential of the relationship beyond recovery. The author has seen therapists so disturbed by the demands of clients that they dreaded the appointment.

The specific limitations required will vary from one therapist to another. One therapist may function perfectly well without a limitation that another therapist requires. The therapist must know himself so that he can decide which limitations he needs in order to function effectively and securely. He must also be able to predict the probable course of the interaction that will follow an action on his part. He must anticipate, for example, that the client may proceed to ask him to drop off his laundry once he has mailed a letter for the client. Will he feel obligated to do so if he sets out on this course by mailing the letter? The giving or accepting of gifts presents similar problems. The first concern when all of these situations arise must be the continuity of the relationship over an indefinite period of time.

The limitations that are required to delineate a professional relationship are more specific. The client may not, for example, inquire into the therapist's personal life. The therapist and client will not go out socially with each other. They will not become friends, business partners or an intellectual team. The time and place of the meetings will be selected to conform to this need for limitations. The interaction between therapist and client will indicate that there is a job to be done for the client and that the therapist is to assist in this undertaking.

Advantages of the group mode of contact. Features of the group contribute to the making of contact, to the continuity of the relationship over a period of time needed for therapy to take place, and to the probability that activation of the approach behavior will result in therapeutic gain.

As has been well demonstrated by social psychologists, the group tends to reduce extreme and deviant associations and to increase common and less personal ones. The effect of the group on the psychotic is not great enough to inhibit all of his highly individual associations, but it does assist the therapist with the problem of making contact and communicating with the client. In a group, he is less peculiar, less deviant, less apt to use his personalized language, and less apt to talk about his delusions or hallucinations than he would be in individual sessions with the therapist. Only for psychotics whose emotional life lies at the very earliest phase of the infantile stage is this effect unobservable. The conformity effect of the group thus contributes to improved rapport of client and therapist in the early phases of the therapeutic process when every improvement that can possibly be made is greatly needed.

Even more important than making contact with the client is maintaining the interaction with him over a long period of time. Since the continuation of the relationship is primarily the decision of the therapist, the difficulty lies in preventing the therapist from rejecting the client. Psychotics are masters at provoking rejection; they are intensely hostile and dependent.

Most people, including the author, find the extreme dependency of the psychotic rather frightening and depressing and tend to react by pushing psychotics away. But the therapist must not do this. The group mode of contact tends to elicit less intense dependency on the therapist and makes it less likely that the therapist will reach the point of rejecting the client.

One of the major ways in which psychotics express their intense hostility is by blocking the efforts of other people to help or influence them. To endure the long silences of the psychotic, his deeply contemptuous behavior, his pouting, his negativism, his extremely slow pace of therapeutic activity is extremely difficult, the author finds, without showing some of the impatience and anger that such behavior elicits. A group of psychotic clients never seems quite so frightening, so frustrating and so provoking. One or several of the group may show the deep resistance to being influenced that only psychotics can show, but unless there is mismanagement by the therapist, the entire group is seldom stalled. The client's power to thwart the effectiveness of the therapist is reduced by the group mode of contact. The therapist experiences a continual progress toward a goal; it is thus easier to be fully accepting of the psychotic in group contact than in individual contact.

The relatively weak activation of approach behavior in the group, which reduces the intensity of the dependency on the therapist and of the hostility toward him is also advantageous. At lower intensity, the client is likely to discriminate better between the therapist's behavior and the behavior he expects. Therapy is dependent on the activation of approach behavior, but this is not sufficient. The activation must be reduced in intensity to the point that the client's total reaction is in part different from the infantile pattern of the approach behavior. Otherwise, therapy does not take place. Therapy is a progressive alteration of patterns, which if activated at high intensity would only be repeated. To the psychotic client, even in a group, the therapist is a most powerful person, much like the mother was; in individual contact he is overwhelming. It is very desirable to enhance the client's relative power through the group mode of contact. In the group he soon experiences the other clients as his potential allies in the battle against the therapist.

Use of individual contacts

In the author's experience individual therapy in the psychotic deviation has not been so successful as has group therapy. Individual contact, however, makes a contribution to the group therapy program. Such individual sessions must not become, or be confused with, individual therapy. The individual contacts are limited to carefully specified goals which contribute to, support and supplement the group experience. These goals are to capture the psychotic client's attention, increase his participation in the group experience, and to overcome some of the limitations of the group experience in promoting growth. The (individual) introductory and review sessions serve the purpose of improving attention and participation. A session aimed at working through a specified problem, a session that provides support for a client waiting for a suitable group, and an appointment made by a client, all serve to broaden the scope of group therapy.

Introductory session. The introduction of a client to a group requires only a brief individual session with him. If the client is unresponsive, incoherent or irrelevant in what he says he is told by the therapist that he will be expected to attend group sessions at a given time and place. The therapist says that he thinks this activity may be of some benefit to the client. Even when the client gives little recognition of appreciating the individual contact, it is important to continue to respect the dignity of the client to the extent of informing and consulting him about what happens to him.

The individual introductory session with a client whose communications are relevant is aimed at moving toward a mutual understanding between therapist and client of how the group experience might be meaningful for the client. The client may, for example, be aware that groups upset him. If so, the therapist may point out that being part of this group might give him increased understanding of these feelings and help him overcome them. The client may admit confusion about, and may wish to understand, the reason that he is being held in an institution. The therapist may point out that joining the group may answer some of his questions in this regard. In addition to expressing some meaningful relationship of the group to the client, the therapist will communicate the idea that the group may not be just what the client needs, but that perhaps it will have some usefulness to him. In this way the therapist prepares for the possibility that the client will not fit into the group and that he may need to be removed. At the beginning, in the introductory session, the therapist structures this possibility as an inadequacy of the group for the client and not an inadequacy of the client for the group. The client is not expected to adjust to the group unless doing so would help him solve some of his problems in getting along with people. The client who expects to get something out of his participation, is encouraged to evaluate his experiences in these terms. Setting the stage for a continual evaluation of progress is a move in the direction of overcoming the psychotic tendency of gross avoidance of self-evaluation. It is the beginning of the therapist's stimulation of the client toward self-criticism. The therapist informs the client of the time and place of the meeting. The client is invited to offer any feelings or thoughts or questions that he may have about the plans. The introductory sessions ends.

Review session. The review session logically follows the introductory session. Many psychotic clients need individual assistance to see that the group experience is meaningful to them. The review session is limited to the evaluation of progress and to current problems and plans for future use of the group. The concern is with such questions as: What does the group mean to the client? What are his reactions to the members of the group? On what problems of his can he work in the group? What does he offer to the group? The therapist takes the lead in relating the group to the client. For a client at an infantile level it would be absurd if the therapist were to leave it to him to find his own reasons for participating in the group. The review sessions provide the therapist with information about the client's conception of the group and his relationships to its members and to the therapist—information that also assists the therapist in understanding the social problems of the client in the community. The frequency of the review meetings depends largely upon the pace of the client's progress. If he is moving very slowly, there is use for only occasional review, which will keep before the client the idea that he is in a training program and should be making some progress. On the other hand, the reviews will need to be more frequent, perhaps every week or every other week, for clients at the childhood level whose relationships to the group and therapist are changing rather rapidly.

The review sessions provide an opportunity for decision on discontinuing the group sessions for a client or transferring him from a group. Frequently the decision can be made a mutual one of client and therapist. The therapist may merely indicate that he agrees with the client that the group is giving him a hard time and that probably this is because the group is not right for the client. He can then either suggest a transfer to another group if one is available or discontinuing and waiting until a more suitable group is available. The review sessions also provide an opportunity for giving specific assignments to a member, which will be elaborated below.

Working-through session. Working through refers to interactions that either aim at clarification of tendencies to react in a specified area, e.g. to women or to employers, or attempts to change behavior in a specified direction. It is the follow-up of the first glimmering new understanding of what is going wrong in a certain kind of interpersonal relationship. It clarifies the behavioral patterns involved, plants with the client the seeds of some ideas about how his behavior should change in order to be more effective, and provides him with opportunities to change his behavior in the context of the therapeutic interaction. The specification of the problem requiring working through may come from either the review sessions or the group sessions. The decision to work through in an individual session derives from the therapist's judgment that the client could not, at present, use the group for working through his problem, that the group is not concerned with the area that troubles the client and probably will not be concerned with it in the forseeable future.

The verbalizations of psychotic clients are so vague that the therapist should always provide the opportunity for working through when the client is able to identify a specific problem. If the problem is of concern to the group as a whole, the working through can take place in the group sessions. The entire group, for example, may become interested in exploring their relationships to employers; each member may wish to express his feelings and ideas, his past experiences, and his expectations of what is likely to happen in the future. The entire group may search together for a better understanding of the problem. When this happens, the role-playing technique can be of great benefit. The group can contribute to setting up specific situations which can be acted out and which will stimulate further feelings and thoughts

on the problem, which in turn may be used to set up more refined role-playing situations.

In contrast to this working through by the group as a whole,
the sessions of the group offer opportunities for a single member
to experiment with changes in his behavior. If a member has
reached the understanding that he would be happier if he were
more assertive, the group session offers a relatively safe situation
in which he may try out various ways of being more assertive. In
the group session the member can observe the impressions that the
therapist and members of the groups have of his behavior change,
and he can discover what feelings the new behavior arouses in
himself. He can then work through the changes in the way other
people respond to him. The major requirement is that a specific
limited behavioral change can be identified.

The review session provides an opportunity for specifying such
goals of limited behavioral change. A special case of this kind is
an assignment from the therapist. The therapist carefully specifies
the behavioral change that is needed and urges the client to use
the group to practice this assignment. The use of this technique
may sometimes retain members in a group that could not otherwise be retained. For example, the author recalls an incident in
which a client was disruptive in the group because of an almost
continual flow of very loosely connected associations. In the review
session he was told that it was valuable to be able to express one's
self, but that it was also valuable to be able to control or delay
self-expression. He was instructed to use the group experience to
practice silence and give the other members a chance to express
themselves. To assist him in this assignment he was offered an
individual session in which he could express himself freely and
without concern for sharing the time with others. The assignment
worked admirably. The client experienced a sense of achievement
at learning to control his verbalizations in the group. The other
clients could more easily participate, and the cohesion of the group
was strengthened.

The major limitation of the group in providing opportunity
for working through is that a member's feelings in a particular
area may come to the fore at a time when they cannot be explored
in the group. One of the important reasons for supporting a

group therapy program with individual contacts is that the therapist thereby avoids the conflict between his responsibilities to the group and those to an individual member. In order to maintain the therapeutic potential of the group sessions the therapist must give priority to the problems of the group as a whole. (This idea will be elaborated in the next chapter in a section on changing the aggregate into a group.) If a member of the group begins to express feelings for the first time which the therapist recognizes are critical or important, the therapist may find it difficult not to encourage and support the member's elaboration of these feelings. There are times, however, when conditions in the group make it imperative for the therapist not to do so. The therapist may then set up individual sessions with the client aimed at going into a limited and specified area.

These individual sessions aimed at working through must be carefully structured. At no time will they be allowed to become individual therapy with its general concern for the client's growth. The therapist might begin such sessions by saying that he has the impression that the client is concerned about his feelings toward his brothers and sisters and about the influence that these feelings may have on his present life. He may then offer the client some time to work through these feelings, but he will limit the individual session to the sibling rivalry problem, referring all other matters to the group. The therapist may use any technique, free association, reflection of feelings or even role taking, that seems to hold promise of assisting in the working through of the specified problem. The individual sessions are continued until a satisfactory solution is arrived at or until there is no further progress. The individual working through sessions are then terminated but review and group sessions continue.

Supportive sessions. If there is no suitable group available or if the decision is reached in the review sessions that a particular group is no longer suitable for a client, then it must be decided whether the client can manage without special assistance until a suitable group is available or whether he needs individual attention in order to prevent deterioration or excessive discomfort. If supportive individual sessions are decided upon, the therapist limits his actions to those that contribute to the general goal of support. The therapist may encourage, advise and praise the client, or may in other ways strengthen his morale while he waits for a suitable group. No effort is made to analyze the client's social relationships or his relationship to the therapist unless the analysis serves to increase the supportive potential of the relationship. The supportive sessions are held as infrequently as possible. They are discontinued as soon as a suitable group becomes available for the client.

Requested sessions. The psychotic client is usually far along in the course of therapy before he can take the initiative in bringing a problem to the therapist. The therapist should encourage the client to take the initiative by making known to the group that he is available to the members for individual talks by appointment. It seems to be very important to psychotic clients to know that they can individually approach the therapist, but it is surprising how infrequently they make use of the opportunity.

Permitting individual sessions by appointment opens the door to increased initiative and participation of the client. It encourages the client to focus his behavior, to recognize his own need and to search out assistance, in contrast to the dependency in which he waits for someone else to discover his need and bring him help. It makes room for greater mutuality of the therapeutic relationship. The therapist may take the initiative and make the appointment or the client may do so. Such an increase in the client's power and control is highly desirable; it counteracts the feelings of severe helplessness that accompany psychosis.

The requirement that individual sessions be limited to a particular problem that cannot receive suitable attention in the group meetings applies to the requested sessions as it does to all individual contacts. When the client comes to the requested session, the therapist can very naturally ask him why he made the appointment. This will introduce the idea that the therapist expects to have a clear focus for individual contacts. After exploring the client's reason for making the appointment, the therapist must decide whether to refer the client to the group session, or to arrange for individual working-through sessions, or that the matter has been adequately handled by the one appointment.

Advantages of open groups over closed groups

In closed groups, all of the members are present in the beginning and no new members are placed in the group as it develops. In contrast, members may begin with an open group; they may withdraw, drop out or terminate one by one, but the group goes on; those leaving the group are replaced with new members. As soon as any original members are replaced, there are always old and new members.

The open group is usually a more practical instrument for the therapist. In most situations, clients are coming to him at all times rather than at a specified time, such as registration at a school. The therapist must either place the client in a group or provide supportive sessions or ask him to wait. The use of open groups means that the client is more likely to get service immediately, which can be a factor in securing his attention and co-operation. Also, the therapist's burden of providing supportive sessions is reduced. In open groups an error of placement is not so damaging as it is in closed groups. Where members are coming and leaving a client's withdrawal or transfer has less of an emotional impact on him. The therapist does not lose the valuable place in the group; he can make use of it for another client.

Even more important than these practical considerations is the strategic advantage of the open group. The purpose of the whole group therapy program is to encourage relationships with peers and with authorities other than the therapist. When new members enter the open group, the old members may be asked to orient them. This gives the old members a status somewhat distinguished from that of the new members. They have experiences which they can use to train the new members. This distinction in status between old and new members is a beginning of differentiation among the members. It stimulates peer interactions. It leads to periodic self-evaluation by the group that would not otherwise take place. When new members enter, the questions are raised of what the group is, how it can be used, what feelings there are toward the group, and whether it is worthwhile.

The major caution to be observed in the use of open groups is to insure that the addition of new members does not prevent the movement of a group to advanced levels. If a therapy group is involved in the analysis of their social relationships, any new member placed in that group must be capable of joining and participating in this advanced activity.

Selection of members and composition of groups

There are very few psychotics who cannot profit from the experience of participating in a therapy group at some time during the course of their deviation. The problem of selection has little to do with the characteristics of the client; rather, it has to do with relating the client to the available groups. It is a matter of having the right group at the right stage of development for a particular client. Yet there will always be some compromise. A client will never be placed in a group that is exactly right for his maximum growth, nor is a particular client exactly what a group needs. The therapist will decide whether the client fits into a group well enough to merit his staying in that group. The therapist may recognize the inadequacies of a group for a particular client, but he may have no other group available that would offer more to the client than does his present group.

A situation where there are many groups in various stages of development is desirable and offers many advantages. It permits a range of choices in the placement of a particular client. Instead of having to decide whether to put the client in therapy, the therapist can decide on placing the client in the most suitable group available. With an observation room adjacent to the one for therapy, it is fairly easy for the chief therapist of an institution to keep informed about what is happening in many groups. He needs to observe only a few minutes of several sessions to follow the course of a group. With information about the available groups and with information about the client, the chief therapist can recommend the group that appears most promising for the client. The final decision belongs to the therapist of the selected group who must accept responsibility for the client's therapy if he admits him to the group.

There are two broad considerations in placing a client in a

group: 1) avoiding the rejection of the client by the group, and 2) maintaining the therapeutic potential of the group. If there is a misfit, the group may only proceed with the therapeutic process by isolating and rejecting the member. If this cannot be achieved by the group, it is blocked and its therapeutic potential for any of the members of the group is destroyed.

Some, trial and error is inevitable in the placement of clients into groups. This fact is stated in the introductory session which anticipates the possibility of transfer to another group or of withdrawal to await a suitable group.

Clients who are hyperactive, acutely disturbed, severely preoccupied, or showing a marked pressure of speech cannot be placed in a group until these characteristics subside. Their behavior would be too disruptive to permit the group to concentrate on its work.

There appear to be some individuals who are so upset and anxious in a group that they cannot profit from the group experience. On the other hand, there are many clients who are bothered by crowds and are thus made somewhat uncomfortable by the group, but if this discomfort does not reach the point of making it impossible for them to learn from the experience, it is not necessary to eliminate them from a group therapy program.

Because placement involves trial and error, it is essential that withdrawal or transfer be easily achieved without traumatic consequences for the client.

There is no need to exclude clients from group therapy on the basis of low intelligence unless they are mentally defective in which case activity groups are probably more suitable. The range of intelligence, however, should not be too great within a group. Clients of borderline and dull normal intelligence are well grouped together. If the group is generally of normal intelligence, some clients of dull normal intelligence may be included. The therapeutic goals must be altered, depending on the intelligence of the group. The more intelligent people have broader, more complicated, more differentiated social relationships and they are more articulate in describing social realities. Thus a group composed of clients of borderline and dull normal intelligence cannot be expected to come to the same degree of understanding of themselves and other people as a group of clients of higher intelligence. Nevertheless, the group experience can help clients of borderline and dull normal intelligence learn to function like people of similar intelligence whose development has been more nearly normal.

Heterogeneity of social background is highly desirable in the composition of groups. It tends to broaden the perspective of the microcosm of the therapy group.

Too great a difference in the developmental level of the clients would interfere with group cohesion. In general, neurotics and psychotics belong in different groups not only because of the wide difference in developmental level, but also because of the vast difference in the pace of therapy. Compared to neurotics, psychotics progress at a very slow rate. To place a neurotic in a psychotic group is somewhat like trying to train a high school student in kindergarten. The basic emotional concerns are too vastly different. There are exceptions. The author recalls one person whose dominant emotional concerns, following an acute psychotic episode, were at an adolescent level. He was placed in a neurotic group and fitted into the group very well.

Critical dimensions of client and group should not differ greatly. It is undesirable to place a client who is incapable of relevant action in a group that is functioning at the childhood level and is actively concerned with interpreting their relationships to the therapist and to each other. The gap between the client's behavior and the group's interaction is too great. The group is likely to ignore and scold and isolate the client in order to proceed with its activity. Otherwise the client would block the group. On the other hand, the same client might be placed in a group that has only recently achieved the goal of relevance. The group would expect the client to respond with relevance, which would be a goal within possible reach of the client. The pace of this group might be slow enough to let the client catch up with the group. To some extent the therapist can help bridge the gap between the client and the group and can exercise some control over the adverse action of the group toward the client. However, the therapist may find it impossible to shelter a client adequately in a group without jeopardizing the therapeutic potential of his relationship to the group as a whole. The client should then be placed in another group; if that is not possible, he should be removed from the group and either scheduled for a supportive session or merely asked to wait until a more suitable group is available.

Discussions and references

This chapter marks the beginning of the shift in focus from strategy to method; from a theoretical conception of the entire range of therapy to the design of a therapeutic program for the psychotic deviation; from the theory of therapy to its practice. Theory and strategy define objectives; method and technique, how to reach them. There are often and usually many ways to reach an objective. What is important is to define the objective so clearly that various ways of reaching it can be tried and compared. The method presented here is the best that the author's experience up to now has taught him. As Alexander (1963) says, methods should be constantly changing. He notes that in no branch of medicine except psychoanalysis have techniques remained essentially the same for fifty years.

The author is fundamentally and unalterably opposed to the idea that at the level of method there is one good therapeutic relationship, as Rogers (1961), Sechekaye (1961) and many other therapists seem to imply. The author's theory requires that the form of the therapeutic relationship vary with the kind of behavioral deviation and with the progressive and orderly changes taking place during the therapeutic process. The author fails to find in the literature any clear affirmation of the principles that in his system, govern the shaping of the therapeutic relationship; nor does it seem to be recognized that careful shaping of the contact is the major way in which the therapist can control his influence on the client. Rare is the report of a deliberate attempt to manipulate the shape and mode of relationship in order to reach specified subgoals, such as the author proposes; perhaps this is so because of the idea that there is one good form of therapeutic relationship and that this must be something similar to what therapists are shaping in practice. The author urges the careful scrutiny of everything that has implications for the form of the therapeutic relationship. For example, Burrow (1963) notes the implication of secrecy of individual contact as compared to group contact. Is it not more likely that historically the choice of individual contact resulted from the then current social climate in which behavioral deviations were disgraceful and had to be hidden rather than from the requirements of the therapeutic problem? Another example: the space, the room, and the furnishings set a tone for the interpersonal interaction. Why not control them, put them to work in reaching the therapeutic objective? With a task so difficult and with human suffering and happiness at stake, can we afford to be careless?

This chapter must not be interpreted as a complete description of the shaping of the therapeutic relationship; the next three chapters describe the progressive alteration of the shape which is brought about by the interactions between therapist and client. This chapter has dealt with decisions made by therapist on the basis of his technical knowledge and his knowledge of himself; the next three chapters will show the progressive change from the therapist making decisions to the client making them. The problems of this chapter were those of the therapist as supervisor; the problems of the next three chapters will be those of the therapist as participant.

The sum total of all the manipulations described in this chapter is to place the therapist in firm control, which gives him the security to permit freedom of expression to the clients. Stierlin (1961) calls this nonexploiting solidarity and believes it is the nucleus of all therapeutic relationships.

Compared with the literature, the elements of this chapter appear quite familiar, but their place and emphasis and function are changed to meet the requirements of the author's objectives. In this new configuration the old elements become new. Fromm-Reichmann (1952) asserted fifteen years ago that it can be taken for granted that a relationship can be formed with the schizophrenic. She attributes failure to the limitations of the therapist rather than the nature of schizophrenia. Her position is similar to that of Wolman (1965, 1966) who finds that "incurable" describes the absence of an able and willing therapist rather than an attribute of the schizophrenic. The author accepts completely and reaffirms

Fromm-Reichmann's perspective that forming the relationship is but preliminary to using it; her judgment that years were lost in the unproductive activity of learning to understand the symbolic meanings of the special language of the schizophrenic; her insistence that the relationship must remain professional, not become personal.

Those who write about the use of groups for therapeutic purposes (Rosenbaum and Berger, 1963; Foulkes and Anthony, 1957; Bion, 1961; Burrow, 1963; Gault, 1953; Bach, 1954; Powdermaker et al., 1953; Hobbs, 1951; Klapman, 1959) report special merits and favorable results with groups. Both Neighbor et al. (1963) and Klapman (1963) describe group therapy as the treatment of choice in some cases. Foulkes and Anthony (1957) affirm that the group offers the only access to some data, that it is more primitive than individuality, and that concepts should be derived from the study of groups rather than individuals. Murphy (1963) likens the group to family support and progressive education. Frank (1963) reports that the tone of interpersonal relationships in a mental hospital became increasingly democratic with the progress of a group therapy program. Rose (1963) sees promise of reducing the time required for therapy through the use of groups. Marsh (1963) and Foulkes (1963) list the special merits of the group for therapeutic purposes.

Klapman (1959) and Rosenbaum (1965) summarize the history of thereapeutic groups; their chapters permit a quick view of the variation of practice.

The effectiveness of group over individual sessions for making contact with the schizophrenic is frequently mentioned in the literature. Speers and Lansing (1965) report that a non-pathological symbiotic relationship is rapidly established with schizophrenic children through the group. Smolen and Lifton (1966) find the group especially effective in breaking the barrier of autism of schizophrenic children. Schilder (1963), Klapman (1963) and Dreikurs (1963), all affirm that the group reaches some individuals whom individual contact would and could not reach. Allport (1955) and Dashiell (1935) report the increase in conformity of thought in a group, as compared to alone. Tate (1957) did not confirm the effect with schizophrenics and hospital aides, probably because a mere aggregate, not a group, was used.

The author places great emphasis on the requirement to maintain, in the therapeutic relationship, the degree of impact adequate to resolve the problem. An impact of half the intensity required is merely wasted effort. Doing therapy is a bit like building a house or writing a book; the job must be completed before the product is of any value. It is the therapist's not the client's responsibility to offer a program capable of reaching a therapeutic objective. Will (1961) specifies the requirement of durability for the therapeutic relationship, but few other therapists do. In the author's system, the probability of the therapist's terminating the relationship or of provoking its termination is reduced by the group mode of contact and the freedom of the therapist to specify limitations. Stierlin (1961) notes that limitations are to help the therapist. The principle of individuation of Wolman (1966) permits the therapist to set his own limits, but no connection is made between this principle and the continuity of the relationship. The matter of organizational supports for the therapist, discussed in the chapter "Achieving Therapeutic Gain," is also a major influence on the continuity of the therapist's participation.

The periodic reviews of progress with the client and the therapist's search for ways of relating the group to the client's interest appears to be new. With this technique the therapist insists on having the clients pay attention. Scheflen (1961) notes the importance of gaining the schizophrenic's attention and credits Rosen with being the first to insist on it in therapy. The therapist, rather than the client, grasps the potentialities of the group, the opportunities it offers, which Standish and Semrad (1963) describe so excellently. Does it not make good sense to have the therapist share his knowledge of these opportunities with the clients? The client may well fail to discover how the group might fit into solving his problem. The author's experience with this technique has been good. He believes that it improves attendance and greatly increases the participation of the clients.

On the matter of selection for group therapy, most reports in the literature consider merely whether various characteristics mean that a client is "in" or "out"—they are not concerned with placement into an appropriate group. The discussion of Foulkes and Anthony (1957) is an exception. They report that a participant who fails to fit in one group may be a great success in another. They also offer the interesting suggestion of allowing the group to make its own selections. Frank (1963) proposes limited range as governing consideration: members should neither be too much alike nor too different. Neighbor et al. (1963) offer very complicated criteria for group membership.

Smolen and Lifton (1966) report a special therapy program for schizophrenic children which appears to be in good accord with the author's approach. The group is the major therapeutic medium; it is supported by individual contacts. The therapeutic relationship is used to build relationships with members. The children are encouraged to relate to volunteers and to those in charge of a day camp. It is reassuring that the program has been found to be beneficial.

The Beginning Phase

Social conditions at the first meeting of the group can best be understood by reference to the developmental scale. Psychotic clients, with rare exceptions, range from early infancy through childhood in the level of their emotional life. The client's reaction to the therapist varies with the level of emotional life. The significance of the therapist corresponds to that of the mother or adult along the developmental scale. For clients in early infancy the therapist has not yet attained dominant emotional significance. For clients in late infancy the therapist has dominant emotional significance which he may use to encourage relationships with other authorities and with peers. For clients at the childhood level the reaction to the therapist is in the process of becoming more limited and realistic. No matter what the level of the psychotic client, the therapist has an emotional significance that vastly surpasses that of members of the group. The pattern of interaction in the beginning will be what has been described as vertical; it will be between two levels of social status. There will be little communication between members. Even messages that are transmitted from member to member will usually be detoured through the therapist.

The degree of weakness of the relationship among members corresponds to that among peers along the developmental scale. The presence of peers is barely a psychological reality for psychotic clients. They are almost insensitive to each other in the group. They seldom greet each other. They make extremely few responses of any kind to each other. They are sometimes very outspoken about not caring in the least what the other members of the group think. They discredit each other in the grossest kind of way. They

127

do not listen to each other. They do not at all believe each other. With a very infantile group of clients, who had been hospitalized for years, the author once spent many sessions in asking each member to give the name of as many other members as he could. The activity demonstrated with great clarity how throughly psychotics ignore each other. It provided a springboard for group attention to the problem of why it was so difficult for them to get acquainted with each other. Their difficulties outside the group in getting to know people and helping people to know them fitted naturally into this discussion.

The way psychotic clients, in a group, ignore each other is due also to the overwhelming significance of the therapist in the group. For the clients to interact directly with each other in the presence of the therapist would be like ordinary citizens talking to each other in the presence of the President of the United States. Only with persistent and total reassurance from the therapist will the group believe that they may respond directly to each other rather than going through the therapist.

Consideration of these social realities leads to the essential conclusion that the group must form around the therapist. The members without the therapist are a mere aggregate of people. The clients' relationship to each other is both weak and unstable. The therapist alone has a position in the group that gives power to bring a group into existence and maintain its continuity. The reverse is also true. He has power to prevent the formation of a group. Finally he has power to shape and mold various kinds of groups. He thus has power to mold the group into the instrument that will serve his therapeutic purpose.

The therapist must provide strong, active leadership in a psychotic group. Reference to the developmental scale will reveal that even at the childhood level, which is the highest level for active psychosis, the formation of a group is highly dependent upon strong leadership. On the other hand, the therapeutic strategy requires that the therapist soften his impact in order to leave room for the development of competence other than his own. It is the consideration of these two somewhat conflicting requirements that determines the form of much of the therapist's behavior.

Graduated goals of the therapist

Some psychotic clients are unresponsive, or incoherent or irrelevant in their talk. These behavioral characteristics arise both out of their infantile emotionality (approach behavior) and the fear and anger generated by years of blocked development (avoidance behavior). When the group as a whole has these characteristics, the therapist will need to give them direct attention before dealing with the social processes in the group. The first goal of the therapist must be to increase the responsiveness of the members to the group situation. This is not a goal that arises out of the group and that is merely phrased by the therapist. It is a goal that the therapist imposes on the situation. Just as it is the mother in normal development who must make contact with the child by playing and smiling and bouncing and making noises, the therapist must initiate contact with the unresponsive psychotic client. Just as the mother watches the child carefully and rewards social responses, the therapist will notice and praise the responses of the psychotic client. Any response is valued above no response. It is necessary first to stimulate the psychotic client to respond to the group situation; then his responses may be gradually molded toward more sociable behavior.

When the group has become responsive the therapist begins to point out the need for coherence and for meaningful, interpretable communication. This is again a goal of the therapist that he imposes on the group. He begins to illustrate how the lack of coherence interferes with making the group sessions satisfying. He may say that he would like to understand, but that he does not. He may ask whether the client could say what he, the therapist, does not understand, in some other way. He may ask if anyone in the group understands the communication so that the therapist gets across the message that no one may understand. In this way the therapist lets the group distinguish between messages that can be understood by someone else and those that cannot. He rewards those messages that are understandable. He shows pleasure and expresses how satisfying it is to understand what another person says. In this way the therapist increases the frequency of coherent messages in the group.

The next and final goal preparatory to social analysis is relevance. The therapist raises the question of how what the client says fits into what the group was discussing. He does not complain too bitterly about messages that do not fit into the topic of the group nor does he reject them, but he does make a distinction, and thus helps the group make a distinction, between relevant and irrelevant messages. By continually making this distinction and by rewarding relevant communications, the therapist moves the group toward coherence and unity: when various members of the group make related contributions toward a topic of interest to the group as a whole. When relevance is attained, the therapist can move the group toward social analysis.

Forming a group of the aggregate

The therapist's eagerness to get on with the social analysis must not prevent him from giving due attention to forming, strenghtening and maintaining the continuity of the group. It must be remembered that the mere simultaneous presence of several clients in the same room is not enough to constitute a psychological group. The therapist must bring unity and cohesion to this aggregate. As he does so, the influence of the group in preventing the highly individual behavior of the psychotic deviation becomes stronger and stronger. The group mode of contact thus becomes progressively more valuable to the therapist in carrying out his strategy.

Several aspects of the therapist's behavior are related to group formation. First, the therapist must, like the leader of any group, interpret the interactions in the group in terms of group feelings, resources and purposes. It is a function of the therapist, which he cannot delegate to a member, to provide a verbal model of the functioning group. The therapist's verbalized interpretations of the attributes of the group bring unity and cohesion to the otherwise disparate actions of the members. The verbal model makes each member's action a contribution to the current group activity or goal.

For example, if feelings are being explored and elaborated, the therapist must not leave it at one member feeling this way, another feeling that way, and a third still another way. The therapist may state that it is interesting to know how the various members feel about a similar problem. This statement makes each member's expression of his feelings a contribution to the group goal of learning how the members feel. The therapist will point out over and over again the special resource of the group: the diverse experience of the members. The therapist will verbalize such group reactions as hesitation in getting started, competition for attention and satisfaction with an achievement. He may point out divisions in the group or sub-groupings. He is the spokesman for the condition and mood of the group. In the fulfillment of this function he brings unity and cooperation to the group.

A second way in which the therapist brings unity to the group is by making explicit statements about the things the members have in common. The psychotic client tends to feel different, alien, separated from people. This feeling is probably a derivative of the long years of blocked, frustrated relations with people and the intense contempt for people that this thwarting has generated. The psychotic client is quick to recognize his difference from the other members of the group and slow to recognize his similarity to them. In part, this is associated with the low level of abstraction associated with his egocentrism. It is especially important for the therapist to point out the common ground shared by the members of the group. They all have problems in living. The psychotic client feels that his problems separate and make him different from other people. The therapist will let him discover that his problems unite him with the group.

Third, the therapist must permit the psychotic clients to exaggerate his potentials, as if he were almost omnipotent without feeling compelled to "set the group straight." The exaggeration of the therapist's power arises out of the long-standing infantile needs of the clients. It is also a function of their desperation. The exaggeration is a demand of the clients that the therapist be as they picture him. The psychotic client undertakes to achieve security by relating himself to a person who has the primitive image of the mothering one. Thus if the therapist insists upon correcting every exaggeration of his potentials, he will merely disqualify himself for leadership of the psychotic group. The author once illustrated this situation to a student therapist as follows: "The group is asking me to play God and I am considering my qualifications for the job." The therapist's careful consideration of the group's implicit demand has the effect of continuing interaction until the group can explicitly state its demand. Reflection and clarification of feelings are useful techniques in making the implicit more and more explicit: the therapist presents to the group with greater and greater clarity the role the group assigns to him and he exposes thereby their exaggeration to the attention of the group.

It should be noted that only the clients have the liberty to exaggerate the therapist's role. The therapist has no such liberty. He must carefully avoid actions of any kind, verbal or nonverbal, that implicitly or explicitly assign an exaggerated role to himself. The group exaggerates the therapist's role to the point of letting him have nearly total responsibility. This is an implication which the therapist must submit to the gradual process of clarification. The therapist will disqualify himself for leadership, if he were to insist that the group attribute to him just a reasonable responsibility. So he will take the attitude that it is clear to him that he has a definite responsibility for the group. Eventually and gradually he will be able to raise the question of what his responsibility is and what the responsibility of the clients is. The division of responsibility among the group members is a matter for prolonged negotiation which in turn, will contribute to the members' growth. The task for the therapist is to permit the members to make him, by their actions, almost totally responsible and then to structure, by his actions, his relationship to the group in a way that permits them to accept a greater and greater degree of responsibility without infringement on his rights or reflection on his honor.

Fourth, the therapist must maintain his relationship to the group as a whole and avoid entering and building an individual one with any member. The group mode of contact requires an entirely different orientation from that of the individual mode of contact. In individual therapy there are two protagonists. It is unnecessary for either to shape his behavior out of consideration for the presence of other people. In the group mode of contact the failure of either therapist or member to take account of the presence of other people takes on special interpersonal meanings, one of which is always offense. It is inconsiderate to others present for two people to carry on a sequence of interactions that does not relate to the group as a whole but only to matters of interest to the two people alone. If in a group situation the therapist permits a dyadic relationship he is in effect doing individual therapy with the one member and is placing all other members in the position of audience. He is exhibiting his expert skill to an audience of psychotic clients, which can only add to their feelings of inadequacy, inferiority and helplessness. In addition, the dyadic relationship within the group will inevitably produce private, intimate material that will embarrass the one member and offend the captive audience.

The absolute requirement that the therapist must not enter a dyad is a major reason for including individual contacts in a group therapy program. With this support available to the client, the therapist may merely remark during a group session that a member could use some individual attention and then make the arrangements. For example, if a member is pushing a matter that the group is not prepared to handle, the therapist may tell him that the matter needs individual handling and thus direct him away from bringing this material into the group. Most of the time a member's efforts to establish a dyad with the therapist in the group sessions is an effort to have a private, personal, special status with the therapist, an effort to be the favorite. This is, of course, a matter for social analysis when the group is ready for this kind of handling. Until such time, the therapist may have to remind the client continually of the presence of the other members of the group. He may ask the member to speak loud enough so that all of the members of the group may hear him; he may ask the client whether what he is saying is of concern to the group as a whole or not; he may define the feeling that is being expressed by the client and ask for similar feelings from the other members. All of these actions of the therapist reflect his awareness of the group situation and call this fact to the attention of the client.

The failure of the therapist to maintain a relationship to the group as a whole is a strategic error; it defeats the purpose of the therapist, which is to encourage relationships among members. If the therapist enters into dyads, he invites a pattern of vertical interactions to the detriment of the desired horizontal pattern. In order to maintain a relationship to the group as a whole, he must search for common ground among clients and point them out, which encourages interaction among clients to explore and elaborate upon them.

Strategic error and disillusionment

With the therapist's leadership, the group as a whole comes to the point of accepting the idea that they may be able to help one another. One of the first signs of this is that a member will tell his story, and then be interrogated by the group and receive its advice. It is important for the therapist to break up this pattern of group interaction in its early form. The pattern is essentially a dyad between the selected member and the remainder of the members as a unit.

There are many things wrong with the pattern, especially for psychotic clients. It tends to single out and enhance the feeling of differentness of the member who is selected to tell his story. The pattern of interaction, apart from the content of what he tells, structures a relationship in which he has problems and the other members of the group will undertake to solve them for him. It does not give recognition to the fact that all of the members of the group have problems. It encourages the idea, already all too prevalent in psychosis, that there are people with problems and that there are people without problems who give help. There is a lack of understanding that people who have problems themselves and who need help in some respects are also able to give help. For maximum effectiveness, the interaction pattern of the group must demonstrate to the member that the feelings that seemed to alienate him from other people are the very feelings that give him a common basis with the group; it is not enough to merely verbalize these ideas. The erroneous interaction pattern promotes the idea that help comes through advice. It ignores the possibilities of help through assistance in self-expression in sharing experiences, and in fulfilling social needs for recognition and encouragement.

If the group offers advice to the selected member, inevitably the result is disillusionment. The advice is usually good; it usually sets a long-range goal. But the member is not prepared to accept the advice. It recommends to him actions that are far beyond his developmental level. When he fails to follow the advice, there is serious risk of an attack by the group on him. The group reacts with anger and rejects the member. At the same time the group experiences disillusionment with the method and feels convinced that the idea that they can help each other is wrong after all.

The therapist will have no great difficulty in breaking up this pattern at its beginning. In order to limit the emphasis on advice, he may initiate discussion about the means by which the group can be of help to each other. If the group selects a member to tell his story, the therapist can always move from the communications of the member back to the group for similar experiences. By his actions, he continues to communicate his understanding that all of the members have their problems, not just this one member, and that there are similarities in the experiences of the members. If necessary, he can explicitly point out that the selected member is not the only one who has problems in living.

The group is not prepared to solve directly any occupational, marital, legal, business or social problems. The group offers opportunities for experiences that promote growth, which improves the quality of the members' solutions of problems in all of these areas. The improvement must be mediated by behavioral development, not by advice on all these diverse matters. The group must not phrase its problems in terms of what to do about lack of money, about a nagging wife or about a legal complaint. The therapist will help prevent this kind of definition of problems by focusing on such problems as difficulty in saying what one wants to say, alienation from people, lack of interest in things, wish to be away from people, avoidance of a responsibility and so on. All of these problems, however, must be gone into as group problems, not as the problems of an individual member.

Tests of the therapist and how he passes

When the psychotic group progresses to the level of relevance, the members begin to show certain responses that may best be described as tests of the therapist. It is essential to the therapeutic progress that the therapist recognize the deep and broad implications of these group actions. If the therapist answers these actions incorrectly, he may destroy his contact with the group or he may structure his relationship to the group in a way that makes it a mere re-enactment of the psychotic development. These tests of the therapist derive very naturally from the history of the psychotic deviation of the developmental process. The tests are expressed through the psychotic's hostility, his ingratitude and his attempts to arouse jealousy in the therapist.

Hostility. The test question posed by the members' hostility might be phrased: Will you continue your interest in me (love me) when I am hostile (bad)? The psychotic deviation with its rejection in fact and in action (but not explicitly) generates an intense, desperate effort to avoid rejection. So much does the psychotic client strive to avoid rejection that he puts his worst self forward first. The aim of this behavior pattern, usually unrecognized by the client, is to insure that if he is to be rejected it will happen at the very beginning, before the relationship means anything to him. Another interpersonal meaning of the psychotic's hostility is the infantile demand for acceptance just as he is without regard to his merit.

Anything approaching warm-blooded, panting anger or active attack has usually been severely punished in the psychotic deviation. For this reason, psychotic hostility seldom follows the pattern of the popular image of the "raving maniac." The more typical form of psychotic hostility is silence, unresponsiveness, not listening, going to sleep, literally turning the back on the speaker and other similar ways of indicating a settled, though emotionally flat, contempt.

How does the therapist pass the test posed by psychotic hostility? He must expect the hostility; he must understand its origin in the psychotic deviation; he must not feel hurt or defeated when it occurs. He must begin with a behavioral expression of concern for the psychotic group, concern that he can maintain in the face of such hostility. His acceptance can take the form of a continuing, stable effort maintained session after session at understanding the members as fully as possible. He must not try to

divert a member from expression of anger. He must not undertake to placate or shame the member. He must not threaten the
member with the bad things that could happen to him if he does
not take a more cooperative approach. He must indicate his satisfaction in knowing exactly and precisely how the member feels.
If this involves anger, well and good; if not, well and good. He
must show satisfaction that the member communicates his feelings
to him. He may indicate that his satisfaction is in the fact that the
member shares his feelings with him and not in the fact that he
feels angry. Coldness and rejection by the therapist in reply to this
initial hostility assures the member that things have not changed:
if he expresses himself, he is rejected. In order to reach his therapeutic objective, the therapist must insure that his warmth and
interest in the member is not reduced by the hostility.

Ingratitude. Often the ingratitude of the psychotic client is
merely another form of his hostility. Some psychotics, however,
have a history of being exploited by the mother. In order to maintain her feeling of worth, the mother has insisted on massive gratitude for her sacrifices in the child's behalf. Her appetite for gratitude was insatiable. The child's failure to provide ample gratitude led to his punishment and rejection. Clients with this history are especially sensitive to any request of the therapist for
gratitude, even for a moderate, normal, reasonable amount. The
ingratitude is usually expressed in a passive form, like that of the
hostility. Not following what is happening in the group, talking
about how much trouble it is to get to the therapy sessions, com-
plaining of receiving no benefits, and demands that the therapist
do something to help may all be expressions of the member's ingratitude.

To pass the test posed by the members' ingratitude the therapist must maintain a constant warmth and interest in them. He
must not show preference for those members, if there are any,
who express appreciation and praise for him over those who are
demanding and scolding. The therapist may reflect the members'
feeling of ingratitude but he must not be overly solicitous. When
the member is ungrateful, too much warmth from the therapist
conveys: "Look how good I am to you while you are nasty to me."
It shames and degrades the client. For this reason the therapist's

expressed intentions to help cannot be too vigorous, but they must be constant. The therapist must expect ingratitude, as he must hostility, and he must not be hurt when he encounters it. He must learn to sustain his feeling of worth by observing the changing patterns of interaction in the group which imply growth on the part of the members and effectiveness on the part of the therapist. The therapist must be certain that he does not require the gratitude of the members in order to sustain his own security.

Therapist's jealousy. The test posed by the members' actions aimed at arousing the therapist's jealousy is but a continuation of the psychotic deviation. The members assume that the therapist, like the mother of the psychotic deviation, is opposed to their gaining satisfaction from any other authority. The action of the members may be either to express how nice someone else was to them, which is hostility toward the therapist, or how much they were abused by their contacts with other authorities, which may be aimed at pleasing the therapist.

In order to pass this test, the therapist must be aware that the reports of the clients represent another attempt in a lifelong struggle to establish relationships with people other than the mother. The therapist must be very careful not to act in any way that could be interpreted as jealousy or as an opposition on his part to the members' relations with other authority figures. The therapist must welcome and encourage full expression of feelings about what other people mean to the member. He must indicate that he regards it as both natural and desirable that the members should relate to other people. The therapist must understand that the clients want to know if he, like the mother, believes that they will always be abused if they relate to anyone other than him. The therapist's answer to this implication is of critical importance because it will influence the structure of the group. If he communicates that his attitudes are much like those of the mother, he tends to establish a group in which he is seen as all-powerful and all-sufficient. And he fails to establish a relationship with the members that is capable of reaching the strategic objective of encouraging and supporting their relationships with other people. The therapist must never imply that he believes the difficulties experienced by the members in relating themselves to other people are inevitable. On the contrary, he must lay the foundation for raising the question of whether the members might use the group to learn how to avoid being abused by other people.

Using the therapist's power to protect values essential to the therapeutic process

Especially in the early stages of group development, the therapist must not hesitate to use his great power to maintain values essential to the therapeutic process. His use of power for this purpose will in general center around two areas: freedom of expression and the therapist's belief in the eventual efficacy of the group.

Psychotic people do not give to each other the freedom of expressing individual opinion. In the psychotic deviation the mother punishes any feeling or opinion that is independent from her own. The reaction of the psychotic client is very similar to that of his mother. He tends to take offense if anyone feels differently about something from the way he feels. It is as if, by feeling differently, the person challenged his competence.

The therapist should use his power to protect a member from strong attack by another member because of a point of view that he has expressed. He should stress the value of everyone being entitled to his opinion. He should emphasize that people feel differently about the same things, and that he is interested in just how each member of the group feels about the things that come up. He should express that one of the reasons for the group sessions is to get the different points of view, that they are a potential source for broader understanding. He should challenge any implication that everybody feels a certain way except crazy people. He should avoid participating in a search for the one right way to feel.

In order to encourage the members to express how they feel, the therapist should avoid expressing how he feels, especially in the early stages of the group. If he expresses his feelings, he tends to cut off expression from the members of the group.

Not only must the therapist use his power to keep members from embarrassing each other in the group sessions, but he must insist also that no member be embarrassed by another member outside the group because of his behavior during the group sessions. The therapist should make it clear that violation of this rule is grounds for dropping a member from the group. The author does this, but he has never actually had to impose this penalty. The group appears to understand the need for the rule and to appreciate the protection that it gives to each of them.

In the beginning the therapist is alone in his belief in the efficacy of the group. The belief is not shared by any member of the group. It is unnecessary and undesirable for the therapist to impose his belief on the members of the group or even to persuade them to accept his point of view. Nevertheless, his actions of constancy and loyalty toward the group demonstrate his belief in its efficacy. He must welcome expression of the members' doubts about the benefits the group offers. He must help through reflection and clarification of feelings to air the doubts fully. If asked by the group for his opinion, the therapist will express his confidence in the potential value of the group to many people. He expresses his opinion on this matter as a means of protecting essential values. He does not express how he feels about politics or religion or social problems or which foods he prefers because his opinions on these subjects would not contribute to the therapeutic process.

Limiting the therapist's significance

In view of the level of emotional development of the clients, the therapist must provide strong leadership and must permit the members to exaggerate his significance in order to strengthen group cohesion. Also, his protection of values essential to the therapeutic process may require actions that tend to exaggerate his impact. Nevertheless, from the beginning, but especially after the group has reached the level of relevance, the therapist's action will emphasize the contributions the members make. He will provide his leadership in ways that express his confidence in the members and that do not imply that he is the only competent person in the group. The implications of the therapist's action are not verbalized until the group is ready, because verbalizing them tends to emphasize the responsibility of the group.

Gaining the clients' consent and commitment. The impact of the therapist is exaggerated by the fact that he has placed many of the members of the group in therapy without their active consent. When the group begins to bring up material reflecting the unpleasantness of having another person's decisions imposed upon them, the therapist may lead the group in a series of interactions that culminate in the group's consent to therapy and their increased commitment of themselves to participation in the group.

The idea of being dominated by another person's decision is usually first expressed in a content that refers to people and places far removed from the group and the immediate surroundings. When the members begin to refer to the institution where they now are and to its personnel, the therapist may anticipate the next step and remark that it must have been unpleasant for members to have been told to attend the group sessions without having been consulted regarding their wishes. He thus opens a discussion of the relationship between therapist and members. He then invites expressions from the group of what their experiences in the sessions have been; of what membership in the group has meant to them. Generally, the group's point appears to be that they want to be consulted about their participation in the group. Usually they are not sure whether the group has been of help to them or not. Most of them do not mind coming to the group. In accordance with his obligation to protect values essential to the therapeutic process, the therapist must clearly indicate that he believes the members' participation in the group can be of some help to them. He strongly advises, but he does not order, that the clients continue their participation in the sessions. At the same time the therapist gives sympathetic understanding to the idea that it is unpleasant to have anything imposed on you and indicates that he would not like to impose participation in the group on the members. The therapist must be prepared, however, not to interfere with the decision of a member who definitely does not wish to continue in the group. The therapist should indicate that he feels the member is making a mistake, that he hopes he will reconsider, and that the door will be open to him if he changes his mind. In the author's experience, if members are permitted to fully express their feelings of being dominated and are guided in a review of what the group means to them, their passive resistance will decrease and their active involvement in the sessions will increase significantly.

Picturing the therapist's accountability. The members interpret the therapeutic relationship as one in which they are completely powerless and helpless, while the therapist maintains an absolute and largely unquestionable control. To the therapist this is a very strange view; he feels he is acting in a highly responsible way toward the group. It may be difficult for him to remember that psychotic members feel that they are accountable to the therapist but that he is not accountable to them. They do not feel that they have a right to ask why the therapist is late for a session or to complain that his absence from a session is disturbing to them. The therapist must give strong encouragement to expressions from the members that bring these assumptions out for inspection by the group. The therapist invites the members to re-examine these assumptions and communicates his willingness to enter a relationship of mutual responsibility and accountability.

Communications along this line help the members to recognize the nature of social contacts. It helps them to understand that not only are employees accountable to an employer but that in some ways an employer is accountable to employees. A child is accountable to a parent, but a parent is responsible for a child. Such recognitions tend to reduce the helplessness of psychotics and to evolve a picture of an understandable, intelligible, controlable, ordered society; they stimulate thought about what the members' obligations are to the various people in their lives and what those people's obligations are to them. Thus, members move toward recognition of the fact that the therapist is their paid assistant who is to help them improve their relationships with other people.

The therapist's entrance. The way in which the therapist enters the therapy room is significant in structuring the kind of leadership he proposes to give. There should be no great distinction between the way he enters and the way the members do. He should come into the room and take a seat and begin listening to what is going on. He should inquire into what was happening before his arrival. Such an entrance avoids the implication that only after the therapist's arrival do important things begin to happen, that what happens before he comes is of no signicance, and that the group is expected to get down to business only upon his arrival. It implies that the members, not the therapist, have something of importance to say, and that the therapist is interested in hearing from them rather than in delivering an important message to them. It tends to emphasize the presence of the members of the group rather than the presence of the therapist.

Redirection of questions. The redirection of questions will tend to limit the awesome power and authority of the therapist and to increase the power and competence of the members. In the beginning, the members will relate to the therapist as if he were the most competent and the most expert in every kind of question and problem under the sun. They will structure a relationship in which he knows more about business, law, medicine, world affairs, construction of submarines, labor-management problems and photography. If the therapist accedes to this structure by attempting to answer questions from all of these areas, he leaves no room for the growth of competence other than his own. The therapist's competence is in interpersonal relations. If the question applies to this area, he may expect to give a more definitive answer than any member of the group. In other areas, he may assume that the members of the group are just as competent as he or more so. By the redirection of questions he makes a start toward getting the clients to interact directly with each other. For a long time they may need to interact with each other through the therapist; but the therapist demonstrates to the questioning member that he can receive help from another member, and he demonstrates to the answering member that he has the competence to be of assistance to other members. Through repeated demonstrations of this kind the members can discover that they may go directly to each other without detouring through the therapist. Because of their long history of punishment for relating to peers, this development will necessarily be slow.

Reviewing the members' feelings and ideas. The therapist will occasionally review how the various members of the group feel about a particular subject. His review is in the vein of: "Did I get this correctly?" In this kind of interaction the therapist is a follower and listener, not a pace-setter and lecturer. His action expresses his confidence in the group. He demonstrates that he regards what the members say as important, worthy of his attention, worthy of his remembering it. He thus uses the prestige that the group gives to him to enhance the worth of the members. The technique serves the grand strategy of therapy in psychotic deviation. By this example, the therapist encourages the members to listen to each other and to regard what the other member says as important. By reviewing and thus valuing what the members say, the therapist encourages interactions among peers.

One caution should be observed. No therapist should use this technique feeling that since he merely reviews what the members are expressing he has no responsibility. The therapist meets his responsibilities for leadership and for management of the therapeutic process by his choice of when and what to review.

Discussion and references

The focus of this chapter is on the therapist as participant in contrast to that of the first six chapters on the therapist as supervisor. It is apparent that the author believes a great deal of preparation is required for the casual entrance of the therapist as participant. His actions must meet standards that are specified by the experience of the members—experience before their eyes, not in their minds. In order to move toward the therapeutic objective, the therapist must not repeat but broaden what has occurred before the eyes of the client up to the time of the therapist's entrance. The objective is to overcome the experiential deprivation of the client.

Bion (1961), in *experiences* 1 and 4, beautifully describes in behavioral terms the initial preoccupation of the group with the therapist. Foulkes and Anthony (1957) note the changes from a mere collection of people to a leader-centered (initial) phase, to a group-centered (intermediate) phase. This differentiation parallels the author's description. The author's phases of therapy follow major shifts in the focus of the interaction and are thus more than arbitrary divisions of a polar variable (Loevinger, 1966). The changing pattern of interaction parallels that of the developmental scale. The leader-centeredness of the beginning phase is again encountered in the final phase, but both content and mode of expression are vastly changed.

The literature has a great deal to say about what the participation of the therapist should be like. Most of these accounts deal with what are, in this author's opinion, the invariant values that are being expressed by the therapist's action. Thus Perry (1961) recommends warmth, concern and openness to whatever the patient brings; Shlien (1961) understanding, acceptance, sharing the client's view of reality; Hill (1955) interest, warmth, helpfulness in the intransitive mood, not imposed or demanding; Arieti (1955) benevolent, sincere helpfulness with no demands. Other accounts deal with the objectives of the therapist's participation. For family therapy, Framo (1965) recommends promoting family interaction and not dealing with symptoms; and Bowen (1965), supporting the separation of the family. Standish and Semrad (1963) describe in common behavioral terms what the therapist should and should not do; the report is an excellent example of the communicative effectiveness of such terminology. Other reports focus on the level of the therapist's activity and responsibility, which, in the author's view, should change during the therapeutic process just as it does, for the parent, during normal development. Rosen (1964) would have the therapist take charge and become a foster parent. Arieti (1961) recommends active, intense, intervention. Shlien (1961) prohibits the therapist from imposing his view of reality on the client or interfering with the client's right of self-determination. Searles (1965, Ch. 22) finds a place for therapist's neutral responses as well as for his emotional reactions. The idea is similar to that of Arieti (1955), that the therapist should not be overly solicitous, to that of Fromm-Reichmann (1952), that the relationship must maintain a professional character, and to that of the author, that the therapist must not be overly kind so as not to cause the client shame and humiliation when he expresses hostility. At a theoretical level, the therapist's participation is described in terms of broad objectives. The psychoanalytically oriented therapy is represented, e.g., by Arieti (1955) and Speers and Lansing (1965) : the therapist must form a symbiotic relationship and progressively bring about individuation and separation. Brody

(1961) tells what the therapist should teach the schizophrenic. Scheflen (1961) has the therapist carry out a program of actions aimed at identification. Sechekaye (1961) would merely have the therapist be a good object.

The strong emphasis on the implication of the therapist's actions in this chapter is characteristic also of the literature. Roessler (1961) pointedly emphasizes gestures over verbal communications. Standish and Semrad (1963) consider actions more valid than words as indicators of the therapist's interest in the patient. Searles (1965, Ch. 19) emphasizes that nonverbal action communications are more readily understood by the schizophrenic, whose thought processes, as Piaget has shown, emphasize pictures and immediate sensory experience.

The essence of all therapeutic interaction is that the therapist presents himself through his actions as one kind of person while the client's actions indicate that he responds to quite a different kind of person. In this sense, the therapeutic process is an identity struggle, in terms of which Wallace and Fogelson (1965) interpret the interaction in family therapy with the schizophrenic. In the author's view, it is not merely a matter of persuading the client to accept another identity of the therapist and thus of himself, as Frank (1961) proposes, but a matter of changing his identity by a planned program of experiences.

The discussion of graduated goals is an instance of the principle of priority of therapeutic potential over efforts to achieve therapeutic gain. Brody (1961) mentions that paying attention to the therapist is the first approach behavior. Scheflen (1961) emphasizes the importance of gaining the attention of the client for therapies that foster identification. The author would not have the therapist learn to speak the special language of the psychotic deviation but rather would have the therapist insist upon the psychotic's speaking the language of the therapist. This is in line with, but probably goes beyond, the observation of Fromm-Reichmann (1952) that ten years were lost in learning to interpret what schizophrenics mean to say. It is in clear contrast to the injunction of Shlien (1961) against the therapist imposing his values on the client. In the author's view, the freedom of the client and his right to self-determination becomes progressively greater with his growth; it is not complete until adult maturity is reached. The interactions that the graduated goals invite are aimed at an increased attention and participation of the client; this is in line with the thought of Foulkes (1963) that creating activity and spontaneity is winning half the battle.

The events described in the section "Strategic Error and Disillusionment" seem to parallel those that happen in the family that selects one member to be ill, to be the scapegoat (Boszormenyi-Nagy and Framo, 1965; Ackerman, 1958).

Standish and Semrad (1963) note that tests of the therapist mark the first stage of therapy with the psychotic. Scheflen (1961) puts responsibility, dependability, understanding, affective involvement and unwillingness to withdraw on the program of the therapist. He emphasizes that rejection is damning at this particular time. He notes that the schizophrenic feels guilty about turning away from the therapist for gratification; the therapist must show him that he does not feel less competent and successful because of his not being all-sufficient to the patient. Will (1961) has the therapist show clarity, dependability, predictability and security. In the author's view, the essential thing is that the therapist show the client that he is interacting with a person who is clearly different from his mother.

Burrow (1963) insists that a group must have an inherent unity, that it is more than a plurality. He as well as Bion (1961), and Foulkes and Anthony (1957) are eloquent and persistent spokesmen for regarding the group, not the individual, as the proper unit and focus. Foulkes and Anthony make clear that the individual is the object of treatment; the group is the agent, which is exactly what the author thinks. Bach (1954) requires the therapist to be group-oriented, not patient-oriented. The author regards the group orientation as a means to an end. The therapist must relate himself to the group in order to bring to the individual clients the experiences of the therapeutic program. For family therapy, Framo (1965) considers the family as the unit, not the individual member, not even the sick member. Hobbs (1951) insists that the therapist must not do individual therapy in the group. Frank (1963) has a great deal to say about cohesion or the degree to which the individuals make a functioning unity. Foulkes and Anthony point out the importance of each member having a place in, and making a contribution to, the group. They do not specifically require that the therapist provide this view for the group. Schilder (1963) notes that the attitudes expressed in a group are variations of a general attitude, but he does not make clear whether it is the therapist's function to point this out.

Standish and Semrad (1963) describe good and poor groups; Bion (1961) explicitly describes good groups, which implicitly identifies poor ones; Will (1961) notes that in successful therapy there is increasing clarity of identities of participants. These leads should be followed up in order to provide the supervisor-therapist with objective indices of when the participant-therapist is on or off course.

The Middle Phase

The beginning phase of group development finds fulfillment in the middle one. The beginning phase aims at 1) meaningful communication, 2) formation of a group that has therapeutic potential, and 3) progressive modification of the relationship between therapist and members in the direction of reducing the therapist's emotional significance to the members. The dominant focus of the beginning phase is the relationship between therapist and member. The shift of emphasis to the relationship between member and member in the middle phase is a major reorientation.

As would be expected on the theoretical grounds of the developmental level of the psychotic deviation, the emotional significance and power of the therapist in the group remains very high. Nevertheless, the application of the principles of contact, discussed in Chapter VI, progressively decreases the significance of the therapist and increases the significance of the members. This change is reflected in a progressive decrease in vertical and increase in horizontal communications.

In the middle phase members may spontaneously and for several minutes interact with each other. There is increasing evidence of their sensitivity to each other. The relationship among them is quite tenuous; it is easily given up. It shows a lack of consistent form, which reflects the absence of any settled concepts of what the members mean to each other or how they may relate to each other. The members still have no serious purpose for each other, nor does one take seriously what the other says. They give to each other very little credibility. The expectation continues that what the therapist says is the source of help. There is perhaps even a feeling that other members are competitors for the therapist's

time and care. There is no feeling of being responsible or accountable to each other. In many ways the interactions of member and
member are like the play of children. They serve the purpose of
permitting the members to experience various forms of social
relationship.

These changes in the social realities of the group necessitate
alterations in the leadership of the therapist. The members are
now communicative and spontaneous enough to do without the
therapist's stimulation. Up to this point he has led them to do
certain things, to conform to standards essential to the therapeutic
process. He can now shift to follow the group. He now observes,
comments on and clarifies matters that are of general interest to
the group. He exploits the members' new sensitivity to each other
to further their development in a way that will be elaborated
below.

Formulating the problem— being misunderstood

In the middle phase, members will begin to communicate their
experiences of being misunderstood by people. The therapist need
only reflect these communications and note the similarity of the
members' experiences of this kind in order to formulate this as a
group problem. Nevertheless, the therapist should encourage full
and detailed elaboration of these experiences and reports of them
from as many members of the group as possible. Also, the therapist should verbalize clarifications of the problem which present
it from many points of view. The substance of these clarifications
would be: Many of you have experienced being misunderstood by
people; you are concerned about what people think of you, how
they feel about you, how you affect people; you are puzzled about
why people treat you as they do; you would like other people to
understand you better. These clarifications are preliminary to,
and give substance to, the therapist's announcement that the objective of the group is for the members to better understand themselves and other people. He will emphasize that this is a problem
for every person and he will note that there is probably no one

anywhere who could not increase his knowledge of this important problem.

It is important in this development that the therapist follow the group and that his formulation be merely recognition of what the group is communicating. He must not get ahead of the group in making these formulations. To recognize another person's problem as he himself presents it is a sympathetic, helpful action. In contrast, to verbalize his problems before he presents them is the role of the prosecutor and task master. To get ahead of the group in these formulations brings about a minimizing and denial of the problem to a degree that is insurmountable. That the therapist follow rather than lead the group in the formulation of the problem of being misunderstood is essential to overcoming the attempts of the members to deny the significance of the problem.

The attempts to minimize and deny the problem of unsatisfactory relations to other people go right along with the communication of experiences of difficulty. A member may angrily say that he does not care what people think of him. That his anger contradicts his denial of concern cannot be pointed out to him yet. The therapist should handle such a denial in the same way as he would an affirmation, by merely reflecting and clarifying the feelings that are being expressed. Elaboration of the problem will bring to the group's attention the facts that demonstrate the significance of other people's opinions. For example, the members will soon stumble on the fact that they are being kept in an institution against their wishes because of other people's opinion of them. They will recognize that they were or were not given jobs because of another person's opinion. They will conclude that the way other people feel about a person is indeed very significant to his success and happiness.

The members as mirrors

The group is now prepared for the therapist to find ways of advancing the member's interest in the problem of understanding how they affect other people. The therapist may observe how helpful it would be to have more information about other people's reaction than is ordinarily available. He may propose that the group be used to obtain information about how one member affects all of the others. He proposes a relationship of member to member in which each serves as a mirror for the other; this is a specific way in which the members can exploit the sensitivity to each other which emerged in the middle phase. Essentially, the proposal is based on the theoretical view, presented in Chapter II, that the psychotic deviation results from a deprivation of experiences with other people so that the information upon which development of maturity depends is lacking. The therapist thus proposes to use the interaction in the group to eliminate this deprivation. He proposes a course of interaction of member with member that will simulate that of child with child in normal development.

There will inevitably be a resistance from the group to the therapist's proposal. However, the interactions in formulating the problem have already brought into focus the great value of understanding one's self and other people better. Thus when the members express their fears of being hurt by a frank and open revelation of their impressions of each other, the therapist can recognize the legitimacy of such fear but at the same time hold up to the group the great value of the objective. It is worth taking some risk of being hurt in order to understand people and one's relation to people better.

Again, it is important that the therapist propose a way of approaching a problem that the group recognizes rather than a problem that he has attributed to the group or that has validity only as the therapist's opinion. Even while proposing a type of interaction for the group, the therapist retains his role as assistant rather than assuming that of taskmaster.

It is probably best to allow the rules for the mirror interactions to evolve from the group experience. The value of permitting each member to say when he wants impressions from the group and which ones will soon become obvious to the group. The group will discover that the member who is told what impression he makes when he did not want to be told is merely angered; no benefit comes of it. The group then will usually evolve the rule that the member shall ask the group for their impressions. This way each member feels more in control of what happens to him, and less helpless and fearful.

In the review sessions it is frequently possible to identify specific problems that a member may then work out in the mirror interactions. All that is required is the identification of a repetitive experience. For instance, the member may recognize that he frequently feels that other people think he is stupid or that they humiliate him. He can be encouraged in the review session to let the group know about such experiences when he has them and ask for the group's impressions. In this way he can learn to differentiate between how he feels that other people feel about him and the actual feelings of other people toward him, between his idea and reality. Such specific use of the group demonstrates to the member its pertinence and value. It stimulates his interest in continuing his participation.

Benefits of the mirror interactions

The ultimate result of the mirror interactions is an ever fuller and more complex contact of the members with each other, which simulates normal development. The therapist must use this broadening of contact as his ultimate criterion of the success of this phase of the therapeutic process. No matter what else is happening in the group, unless the relationship of member to member is broadening, therapy is not taking place. This general objective and criterion of progress, however, is not adequate to guide the therapist in his leadership in this phase. The following are some ideas about the mechanisms by which the therapist brings about this broadening relationship.

The interactions of mother and child in the psychotic deviation have associated fear and shame with the interactions of the child with his peers—fear because the mother has warned him of abuse and treachery; shame because she regards the child's relations to peers as disloyal. The mirror interactions provide the means for re-conditioning the members; increasingly they make clear the contrast between the attitudes of the therapist and the mother. The therapist has proposed that the members relate themselves to each other; he obviously approves. He is there to work out any difficulties that arise in their relating to each other. He gives no indication of being threatened or of being jealous of the relationship of member to member. These aspects of the interaction of therapist and members lead toward positive affects about contacts with people and toward changing behavior from avoidance to approach.

The two basic questions of the mirror interactions are: 1) How do I impress you, and 2) Why do I impress you that way? These two questions lead very naturally into discussions of communication. The first question leads to identification of errors and problems in sending messages; the second question to identification of errors and problems in receiving messages. The two questions produce material that amply demonstrates the complexity of making oneself understood and understanding other people.

The discussion of problems of communication will include identification of some of the patterns of defective communication that are characteristic of the psychotic deviation. One common pattern is the failure to do anything at all in the direction of learning to communicate effectively. The psychotic tends to feel that other people should know automatically what he wants and how he feels without his having to bother to tell them. He often feels great anger that his needs are not known and responded to unless he has made them known. Another common error is the transmission of a false image of himself. He acts as if he did not care to associate with other people; he may even show annoyance at the intruder. People respond to him on the basis of the message that he transmits: they leave him alone. He, in turn, feels frustrated that his loneliness is not understood by other people. Still another common pattern of the psychotic is his insistence on being accepted according to his own interpretation of himself. He says that he is normal; he expects everyone to accept his interpretation and respond to him accordingly. The discussion of the problems of communication will tend to show how unreasonable this attitude is. It will make clear that people form their impressions from a great deal more than just what is said.

The identification of defective patterns of communication is a first step toward their correction. Once they are identified the group provides an opportunity for practice in correcting them.

The therapist's support and encouragement of this practice tends to bring about a steady improvement.

The knowledge of what is going wrong with communication stimulates ideas about how it might be controlled. The idea that it can be controlled contributes to a willingness to accept responsibility for it. Thus knowledge tends to replace the old attitudes of helplessness and being at the mercy of other people with attitudes of being responsible and in control. The knowledge also tends to reduce the confusion that is so common in the psychotic deviation. It helps the psychotic to make sense of his past experiences. He can now understand better why people had the impression of him that they did and why they acted toward him as they did. He is progressively less confused by his interpersonal experience and therefore increasingly willing to enter into interpersonal relations.

During the mirror interactions the members will learn a new system of values associated with peer relationships which is in contrast to the system of values generated in the mother-child relationship. At first the members will transfer the values of the mother-child relationship to that of peers. Much of the resistance to the mirror interactions may be understood in terms of such a transfer. To overcome the resistance the members must differentiate between the peer relationship and that of mother and child. Impressions the child receives in the mother-child relationship are serious; they are laws; they are definitions of reality and revelations of irrefutable values; they bring with them pressures on behavior. In contrast, the peer relationship generates the frivolous and playful attitudes of interpersonal exchange; their absence in the psychotic deviation is notable and is often noted.

The first reactions of the members to the impressions offered about them will demonstrate an overly serious attitude. This may appear to contradict the idea that the members give to each other very little credibility, but it is probably the same thing from a different viewpoint. Either what one says is true (as in the mother-child relationship) or what one says is of no significance (as in the peer relationship). The therapist has proposed a type of interaction in which the members should listen to what they say of each other. At first the members can understand his proposal only in terms of their past experiences. Bringing into focus the overly serious regard for the mirror interactions, in effect, will show the interpretations to be tenuous, limited, hypothetical, probable—simply points of view, in contrast to the absolute.

The values of the peer relationship become a welcome relief from those of the mother-child relationship. Thus the major problem of the therapist in getting peer interactions going is to bring about an appreciation of the contrast and to help the members work through the inhibitions acquired in the course of the psychotic deviation. Once peer interactions acquire the appropriate values, they tend to be self-perpetuating.

Perhaps it is the devaluation of impressions that takes place during the mirror interactions that enables the members to become better listeners. Since what is said is not of such life or death significance as had been thought, it can be listened to. As the members become better listeners, they are increasingly more influenced by each other and, in general, by people, with whom they come in contact. They become less distant, isolated and alien; they are gradually more like other members of the community.

The members as judges

It is unnecessary to wait until all of the benefits of the mirror interactions are realized before moving on to the next type of interaction: the judging interactions. While the members continue to pay some attention to the giving of impressions of each other, they learn to make judgments of each other. When spontaneity is good in the group and when the members are generally able to take a playful attitude toward impressions (i.e., there are usually no prolonged emotional responses to either giving or receiving an impression), the therapist may permit the beginning of the judging interactions.

In the beginning the members will confuse the giving of impression with judging. An impression deals with the more or less immediately observable: how someone is behaving in the here and now, whether he is aloof, oppositional or cooperative; whether he is friendly or frightening; whether he is forbidding or inviting. The appropriate attitude toward impressions is a playful one.

Judging is a far more complex operation. It requires the combing of many observations that are temporally separated; it requires the use of these observations to make a number of inferences; it requires the comparison of these inferences with one's standards of what is good and bad, adequate or inadequate, worthwhile or useless and such. The therapist will help the members learn to distinguish between impressions and judgments during the mirror interactions. He will ask that the members deal only with the question of how they see each other and that they hold for a later time the question of evaluation. Thus when the group is ready to move into judging interactions, the therapist will need only to announce that he believes the group is now ready to raise questions requiring judgment and direct the attention of the group to the questions that are raised.

The first questions raised usually deal with such matters as whether the members are ready to leave the institution, to handle a job, or to resume the care of home and children. In guiding the group in their consideration of these questions, the therapist can easily ask: What do employers expect of employees? How would the neighbors feel about a member of the group? What makes a good wife or husband? The questions lead quickly into matters of standards and values.

Resistance to judging will go right along with the activity. Much of the benefit of this phase is achieved by the exploration of the resistance. The strongest resistance comes from assertion of the incompetence of the members to make the judgments. The members will usually attempt to refer all questions of judgment to the therapist; they reveal that they continue to believe that only the therapist is competent. The therapist must not deny his competence to make judgments. He probably should not even attempt to make any comparison of his competence with that of the members. He should merely respond that he may on occasion wish to give his judgments about matters that come up but that he believes it would be beneficial for the members to make judgments of each other. He thus encourages a new and more responsible type of relationship between member and member.

Though the quality of the individual member's judgment may be poor, the judging interactions *per se* will promote the psychological development of the members. The value of these interactions lies in the demonstration and elucidation of the judging process rather than specific judgment proffered. On the other hand, the author has never seen a psychotic group reach agreement on a poor judgment. If the group as a whole agree, the judgment is usually as excellent as anything that could be offered by a qualified staff.

Benefits of the judging interactions

The members' experiences during the judging interaction simulate, and substitute for, the experiences that in normal development are encountered upon entering school. Each member is subjected to and must find security among different systems of value, some of which are very foreign to his own. At this phase of group development, it becomes important that the group is composed of members who have heterogeneous social backgrounds. Only diversity will bring the existence of values into focus. The values of the home seem natural, God-given, irrefutable and absolute until they are confronted with the many systems of value in a community.

In general terms, the objective of the judging interactions is to stimulate the development of an adequate concept of the social order. Differentiation is the key process. Just as the infant expects the mother to satisfy all of his needs, the psychotic person expects to participate in a simplified social order. The judging interactions lead to an understanding of the many social roles found in any community. One reason for the social ineffectiveness of the psychotic is his failure to differentiate these social roles. He tends to tell his physician about his need for a job and to tell a potential employer about his aches and pains.

In the analysis of the members' judgments of each other many principles will become clear which are like revelations to the psychotic and which permit him to determine the worth or validity or extent of application of a judgment. The movement is again from the absolutes of the mother-child relationship to the relativity of the relationships in the child-community. The members will learn that the quality of a judgment is dependent upon the relationship between the judge and the person being judged. It is an evaluation from a particular viewpoint. The employer applauds and rewards dedication to a job. The same behavior is condemned if viewed by the marital partner. It will become clear that a judgment reveals as much about the person making it as it does about the object of the judgment. Inherent in the judgment is the value system of the judge. In making judgments of each other, the members of the group reveal their standards, which provides an opportunity for testing and modifying and retesting values in a social context. In the psychotic deviation the individual has never submitted his values to such a test. He either does not know what point of view to take about a matter or he takes a very arbitrary point of view and will not consider the evidence. Only by experiencing this social exposure of his values and by modifying them and retesting them can he develop values in which he puts confidence. He comes to understand that the absolute and universal acceptance that he has been looking for is an impossibility in a social order that is divided up and specialized.

The focus of judging interactions is on the modification of the relationship between member and member. Movement is in the direction of defining the participants as both more responsible and more competent, and this will bring out all the uncertainties of the members about acceptance of responsibility and all their doubts about competence. The working through of these feelings is essential to the growth of the members. The very act of making judgments that are heard and considered increases the feeling of competence of the members, for only competent people make judgments. Modification of the member-to-member relationship necessarily changes that of member to therapist. The interactions define each member as having a degree of competence, a definition incompatible with the old concept of the therapist being the only competent person present, the only one competent to judge the competence of the members. Now they are engaged in establishing their own competence among the members of the group. The judging interactions move the group toward the pre-adolescent level with its system of values of peers in contrast to that of authorities. These developments again reduce the significance of the therapist; but this time that significance is not specifically under consideration.

Discussion and references

Carrying out the program of the participant-therapist in the beginning phase is hard work. It requires careful scrutiny of every action. Mistakes can be and usually are costly. To be the center of communication and to be so grossly distorted is stressful. In contrast, the middle phase is fun. The spotlight is off the therapist. The member-member interactions take on the quality of play. No longer is the therapist a task master imposing his goals on the group; he is now an adult advisor, assisting the group in reaching the goals that it sets for itself.

Malone (1961) mentions that he approaches the schizophrenic as he would a three or four year old child, surely somewhat playfully. Searles (1965, Ch. 18) describes the child-like playfulness he experiences in working with schizophrenics.

The author bases the techniques described in this chapter on the theory of experiential deprivation. In psychotic deviation the individual by-passes the experiences of playful interactions with his peers in infancy and childhood and the more serious interactions with his peers in pre-adolescence and adolescence. The techniques of this chapter are designed to present these experiences belatedly to the person. The vital significance of these interactions for normal growth is documented in the studies of Piaget (Flavell, 1963) and Harlow and Harlow (1962).

The importance of the therapist's emotional reactions to the progress of therapy with the psychotic individual is generally recognized and variously described in the literature. Fromm-Reichmann (1952) mentions that the schizophrenic must be shown not only what was done to him but also what he has done. The mirror interactions are specifically aimed at informing the members of how they affect other people and why they affect them that way. Scheflen (1961) speaks of the therapist giving the patient an image of himself in positive reaction to the patient. Slavson (1963) emphasizes the importance of opportunities for corrective identification. The focus is on relationships as they exist among children.

The therapist's action is aimed at encouraging these relationships. Foulkes and Anthony (1957) speak of corrective experience and ego training. Searles (1965, Ch. 22) sees the therapist's emotional reactions as an aid to differentiation. Arieti (1955), as do many other therapists, specifically aims at the goal of assisting the schizophrenic in establishing communications and forming relationships with others. This is the goal and achievement of the middle phase of therapy.

The Terminal Phase

The beginning of the terminal phase is signaled by actions of the members aimed at identification with the therapist. The two great processes up to this time, i.e., limiting the significance of the therapist and strengthening the competence and identity of the members, lead naturally into the identification interactions. The concern with social rule, with standards and values, and with identity ultimately will focus on the therapist. What kind of person is the therapist? What does he believe? Am I like him? These are the basic questions. To offer leadership in the exploration of these questions is the major function of the therapist during the terminal phase.

The achievements of the judging interactions make possible the identification that takes place during this phase. The concept of the therapist now has a limited form. He has lost his status as a god. He is heroic: he has helped more clients than have ever actually consulted him. He knows a great deal about many things that have never captured his attention. Even so, the members begin to speculate that he may have limitations, which, with proper handling by the therapist, they will assert with increasing confidence and decreasing emotional upset. How the therapist reacts to these beginning speculations is critical to achievement of the benefits of this phase. He must not feel offense that the members attribute limitation to his skill, knowledge and even emotional stability. He must communicate that he regards the members as not basically different from himself.

The individuality and identity of the members of the group are readily discernible in the terminal phase. The judging interactions resulted in the discovery and definition of differences and in an emotional tolerance for them. The relations of member to member during the terminal phase shows considerable stability. There are few returns to the old pattern of relating to each other through the therapist, and there is little need for the therapist to support and encourage interactions between members.

The main focus of the interaction during the terminal phase is again the relationship of member to therapist. The interaction must modify this relationship in the direction of decreased subservience of member to therapist. The member must take the final steps toward feeling, thinking and acting as the equal of the therapist.

The members are free of active psychotic symtoms. The behavioral organization achieved during the judging interactions is incompatible with such behavior as hallucinations, bizarre ideation, feeling of irreality and of alienation from people.

Identification interactions

The identification interactions will bring to light and deal with the various distortions of the identification process so that each member may form a concept of likeness to the therapist that permits the full expression of the members' identity and individuality.

One distortion is a degradation or devaluation of the therapist. The aim is to bring the therapist down to a size that the member can aspire to. The member overdoes it; he goes beyond what he intends. In the face of such a devaluation the therapist must be able to maintain his dignity. He must help the member come to understand that he is reacting to his own inflated concept of the therapist. Another distortion is an overly forward behavior of the client who pushes aside all doubts and acts with unrealistic assurance that he is indeed like the therapist. Or the distortion may be conformity, a giving up of independent beliefs and actions in order to be the same as the therapist. In this distortion the client fails to achieve an identification in abstract terms. Another distortion is the rebellious reaction, which denies any impulse to cooperate with the therapist and exaggerates differences. Still another distortion is the inferiority reaction, a protest that one is not worthy of being like the therapist. Here the client aims to force reassurance from the therapist, to perpetuate his dependency on the therapist. The therapist must assist the group in working through these or any other reactions that block the members from moving in the direction of equality with him.

To help the group reach the objectives of this phase, the therapist may give them more information about himself than he has in the past. In particular, he may raise the question of the limitations of his own competence. When the members express their views on it, he might tell them the experiences that he has had that are pertinent and assist them in coming to accept his limitations. It is the final step in helping the group understand that no one has universal competence and that there is room for each member of the group to lay claim to competence in a limited area without offending either the other members or the therapist. It is a way out of the conflict between loyalty to the therapist and the wish for competence and independence. It is no longer necessary to destroy the therapist in order to establish one's competence.

In the course of coming to appreciate the therapist's limitations, the group is likely to suggest that the therapist may at some time himself need a therapist. This observation will seem funny to the group because of its contrast to the heroic concept. The speculation gives the therapist the opportunity not only for helping the group gain fuller understanding of his limitations but for desensitizing the members to the need for psychological treatment. The therapist may communicate his beliefs that behavioral difficulties can confront anyone, and that for a therapist to need a therapist is no more unusual than it is for a physician to need a physician, or a lawyer to need a lawyer. The therapist might explain, too, that his responsibility for the group has kept him from talking about himself and his problems and his doubts or fears or unhappiness. But the fact that he has not talked about these things to the group does not mean that he does not face them.

Non-verbal communication of attitudes and feelings between therapist and members remains as important as it has been through the whole course of therapy. A member may test the therapist's willingness to accept him as an equal by the way he sits next to him or the way he walks down the hall with him. Assured of his acceptability as an equal, the member walks exactly at the side of the therapist, keeping pace with him, maintaining rapport. It is not necessary to put feelings of pride into words. But it is essential that the therapist welcome the members' gestures of equality.

One function of the therapist during the identification interactions is to assist the members in being like him in abstract and even in symbolic terms rather than concrete ones. The risk of the therapist's revealing his feelings and beliefs to the group is that the members will block expressions of themselves in the interest of being exactly and literally like the therapist.

As in the preceding phases of therapy, the therapist must not make the group move too fast. The group must move step by step so that they can activate the emotions that either block or distort their identification with the therapist. In trying to move too fast the group inevitably acquires a lot of verbal propositions that have no validity in their emotions. They must move at a pace slow enough to permit full participation of feelings.

The question of termination of therapy fits naturally into the identification interactions: Is the member really the equal of the therapist and ready to give up a dependenty relationship to him? The author believes that the therapist is competent to answer the question and has, therefore, a degree of responsibility. He cannot reasonably leave to the client full responsibility for terminating therapy. The member is entitled to know the therapist's opinion on the question if he asks for it. If he undertakes to terminate therapy when the therapist does not believe he is ready, the therapist should tell him his opinion and advise him to continue therapy even if the client does not ask for the opinion. If the therapist believes a client is ready for termination and that client does not bring up the question, the therapist should do so. The therapist should make use of his power to advise the client in order to prevent a termination that has the quality of "If I don't do it now, I'll never do it." The therapist can point out that it is not too important whether termination occurs today or next week. If the client should find after termination that he needs further assistance from the therapist, the door will be open for him to return. The act of termination should be as simple and natural as two friends saying good-bye.

Benefits of the identification interactions

The identification interactions establish the status, security and pattern of interaction typical of adults; they define what adulthood means and define the members of the group as belonging to this class. Movement is in the direction of broader, more complex, and more effortless social relationships. It is a process of liberation from the concept of the closed society that the interactions with the mother had defined. Now the interactions convey the authority for assuming an adult role. The members discover that they are not required to take a subservient role in relation to authority.

From the perspective of this phase, the process of limiting the concept of the therapist can be viewed as gaining step by step an adequate concept of what an adult is like. It is not the therapist as an individual that the members are trying to understand; it is the therapist as an adult and an authority. While the questions of this phase have to do with what the therapist is like, they are in actuality questions of the identity of the members as defined by a comparison of client to therapist. The limitation of the status of the therapist and the strengthening of the member's status bring closer and closer together the concepts of adulthood and self. The identification interactions provide the final test of whether these two concepts belong to the same class.

The effectiveness of the members in pursuing ordinary social objectives, of business and pleasure, is increased by the achievements of this phase. The question of one's relationship to adulthood disrupts the pursuit of other objectives until it is resolved. Even if members enter activities of a practical kind, the effort to resolve this issue dominates over pursuit of the ostensible activity. Distortions of the identification process have the effect of perpetuating the issue unresolved. During this phase of therapy the question of one's adulthood must change from that of a hotly debated issue to one of a settled agreement. It is a change from having to make a point of one's adulthood to merely assuming that it is there, and that it is generally understood and accepted and thus has social validity. It is this change that produces the decrease in the strain of behavior.

It is during this final phase that the therapist's retention of expertness and authority through all previous phases of therapy becomes critical to the achievement of therapeutic gain. It is now essential that he has not, in the interest of establishing contact, become "one of the boys." The identification interactions require that the therapist certify the adulthood of the members. His action at this time must convey an invitation to the members to step up and share his status; he must not have stepped down at any time to their status. Only an adult can authorize a person to regard himself as an adult.

With the ending of the identification interactions, the emotional life of the member has at last caught up with his physical development. The blocks of his fulfillment of himself have been removed; he is free to be all that he is capable of being, to be himself.

Discussion and references

As in the beginning phase, the focus is back on the interactions between participant-therapist and member. The difference in content of the two phases is vast. In the beginning phase, the members center on the therapist, demanding that he be an all-sufficient god and relieve them of all active encounters with the environment. In the terminal phase the members ask the therapist to recognize and certify their adulthood.

Scheflen (1961) affirms the belief that all therapists work in part through identification. He reviews the literature for similar ideas and offers broad guidelines for such a therapeutic program. The author believes that identification becomes the critical and stage-specific issue of the end of therapy. The goal of encouraging identification does not adequately describe the entire process. Scheflen takes notice of the problem of concrete identifications with the therapist and recommends encouraging the patients to identify with institutions and abstractions.

Brody (1961) believes the most important insight achieved by the patient is the recognition of his similarity or identity with the doctor. Hill (1955) speaks of the patient taking qualities from the physician that he likes. He recognizes that for successful termination of therapy it is important to leave the door open for the patient's return.

Searles (1965, Ch. 24) agrees with the need of the patient to identify and reviews the concurring literature. He makes the important point that the efforts of the patient to identify may be reacted to as competition. In the author's view, this is especially likely to happen if the therapist conceives of himself as in some way fundamentally different from the client. Perhaps unfortunately Burrow (Gault, 1953) said that both therapist and client were sick rather than that the two were not fundamentally different. Thus, his enduring contribution of viewing therapist and client as more alike than different has not yet been fully appreciated by many therapists. As he said, and as should be apparent from watching them work together, they are both members of the human species.

References

Ackerman, N.W. *The Psychodynamics of Family Life: Diagnosis and Treatment of Family Relationships.* New York: Basic Books, 1958.

Ackerman, N. W. Psychoanalysis and group psychotherapy. In M. Rosenbaum & M. Berger (Eds.), *Group Psychotherapy and Group Function.* New York: Basic Books, 1963, pp. 250-260, (orig. pub. 1949).

Alexander, F. *Fundamentals of Psychoanalysis.* New York: W. W. Norton & Co., 1948.

Alexander, F. The dynamics of psychotherapy in the light of learning theory. *Amer. J. Psychiat.,* 1963, *120,* 440-448.

Allen, F. *Psychotherapy with Children.* New York: W. W. Norton & Co., 1942.

Allport, F. H. The influence of the group upon association and thought. In A. P. Hare, *et al.* (Eds.), *Small Groups: Studies in Social Interaction.* New York: Alfred A. Knopf, 1955, pp. 31-34, (orig. pub. 1920).

Arieti, S. *Interpretation of Schizophrenia.* New York: Brunner, 1955.

Arieti, S. Introductory notes on the psychoanalytic therapy of schizophrenics. In A. Burton (Ed.), *Psychotherapy of the Psychoses.* New York: Basic Books, 1961, pp. 69-89.

Bach, G. R. *Intensive Group Psychotherapy.* New York: Ronald Press Co., 1954.

Benedek, T. Parenthood as a developmental phase. *J. Amer. Psychoanalytic Assoc.,* 1959, 7, 389-417.

Bergmann, G. & Spence, K. W. Operationism and theory construction. In Marx, M. H. (Ed.), *Psychological Theory.* New York: The Macmillan Co., 1951, pp. 54-66, (orig. pub. 1941).

Bindra, Dalbir. Components of general activity and the analysis of behavior. *Psychol. Rev.,* 1961, *68,* 205-215.

Bion, W. R. *Experiences in Groups.* New York: Basic Books, 1961, (orig. pub. 1948-1951).

Boszormenyi-Nagy, I. A theory of relationships: Experience and transaction. In I. Boszormenyi-nagy and J. L. Framo (Eds.), *Intensive Family Therapy: Theoretical and Practical Aspects.* New York: Harper & Row, 1965, pp. 33-86.

Boszormenyi-Nagy, I. & Framo, J. L. (Eds.) *Intensive Family Therapy: Theoretical and Practical Aspects.* New York: Harper & Row, 1965.

Bowen, M. A family concept of schizophrenia, In D. D. Jackson (Ed.), *The Etiology of Schizophrenia.* New York: Basic Books, 1960, pp. 346-372.

Bowen, M. Family psychotherapy with schizophrenia in the hospital and in private practice. In I. Boszormenyi-nagy & J. L. Framo (Eds.), *Intensive*

Family Therapy: Theoretical and Practical Aspects. New York: Harper & Row, 1965, pp. 213-244.

Berger, L., *et al.* Learning theory and behavior therapy: A reply to Rachman and Eysenck. *Psychol. Bull.,* 1966, *65,* 170-173.

Brody, E. B. What do schizophrenics learn during psychotherapy and how do they learn it? In J. G. Dawson, *et al.* (Eds.), *Psychotherapy with Schizophrenics: A reappraisal.* Baton Rouge: Louisiana State University, 1961.

Brody, E .B. & Redlich, F. C. (Eds.) *Psychotherapy with Schizophrenics: A Symposium.* New York: International Universities Press, 1952.

Brunswik, E. The conceptual focus of systems. In M. H. Marx (Ed.), *Psychological Theory.* New York: The Macmillan Co., 1951, pp. 131-143, (orig. pub. 1939).

Burrow, T. The group method of analysis. In M. Rosenbaum & M. Berger (Eds.), *Group Psychotherapy and Group Function.* New York: Basic Books, 1963, pp. 143-153, (orig. pub. 1927).

Burton, A. (Ed.) *Psychotherapy of the Psychoses.* New York: Basic Books, 1961.

Clausen, J. A. & Kohn, M. L. Social relations and schizophrenia: A research report and a perspective. In D. D. Jackson (Ed.), *The Etiology of Schizophrenia.* New York: Basic Books, 1960, pp. 295-320.

Cohen, Mabel B. Countertransference and anxiety. *Psychiatry,* 1952, *15,* 231-243.

Dashiell, J. F. Experimental studies of the influence of social situations on the behavior of individual human adults. In C. Murchison (Ed.), *Handbook of Social Psychology.* Worcester, Mass.: Clark University, 1935.

Dawson, J. G. Discussion by Joseph G. Dawson, Ph.D. In J. G. Dawson, *et al.* (Eds.), *Psychotherapy with Schizophrenics: A Reappraisal.* Baton Rouge: Louisiana State University, 1961, pp. 118-122.

Dawson, J. G., *et al.* (Eds.). *Psychotherapy with Schizophrenics: A Reappraisal.* Baton Rouge: Louisiana State University, 1961.

Dreikurs, R. Group psychotherapy from the point of view of Adlerian psychology. In M. Rosenbaum & M. Berger (Eds.), *Group Psychotherapy and Group Function.* New York: Basic Books, 1963, pp. 168-179, (orig. pub. 1957).

Erikson, E. H. *Childhood and Society,* (Rev. ed.). New York: W .W. Norton & Co., 1963, (orig. pub. 1950).

Eysenck, H. J. (Ed.) *Behavior Therapy and the Neuroses.* New York: Pergamon Press, 1960.

Fenichel, O. *The Psychoanalytic Theory of Neurosis.* New York: W. W. Norton & Co., 1945.

Fiedler, F. E. A comparison of therapeutic relationships in psychoanalytic, non-directive and Adlerian therapy. *J. consult Psychol.,* 1950, *14,* 436-445.

Flavell, J. H. *The Developmental Psychology of Jean Piaget.* Princeton: D. Van Nostrand, 1963.

Ford, D. H. & Urban, H. B. *Systems of Psychotherapy*. New York: Wiley & Sons, 1963.

Foulkes, S. H. Group analysis in a military neurosis center. In M. Rosenbaum & M. Berger (Eds.), *Group Psychotherapy and Group Function*. New York: Basic Books, 1963, pp. 469-476, (orig. pub. 1946).

Foulkes, S. H. & Anthony, E. J. *Group Psychotherapy: The Psycho-analytic Approach*. Baltimore: Penguin Books, 1957.

Framo, J. L. Rationale and techniques of intensive family therapy. In I. Boszormenyi-nagy and J. L. Framo (Eds.), *Intensive Family Therapy: Theoretical and Practical Aspects*. New York: Harper & Row, 1965, pp. 143-212.

Frank, J. D. *Persuasion and Healing: A Comparative Study of Psychotherapy*. Baltimore: Johns Hopkins, 1961.

Frank, J. D. Group therapy in the mental hospital. In M. Rosenbaum & M. Berger (Eds.), *Group Psychotherapy and Group Function*. New York: Basic Books, 1963, pp. 453-469, (orig. pub. 1955).

Freeman, H. The current status of behavior therapy. *Compr. Psychiat.*, 1965, *6*, 355-368.

Fromm-Reichmann, Frieda. Some aspects of psychoanalytic psychotherapy with schizophrenics. In E. B. Brody & F. C. Redlich (Eds.), *Psychotherapy with Schizophrenics: A Symposium*. New York: International Universities Press, 1952, pp. 89-112.

Gault, W. E. (Ed.) *Science and Man's Behavior*. New York: Broadway House, 1953.

Gottschalk, L. A. & Auberback, H. (Eds.) *Methods of Research in Psychotherapy*. New York: Meredith Publishing, 1966.

Grossberg, J. M. Behavior therapy: A review. *Psychol. Bull.*, 1964, *62*, 77-88.

Harlow, H. F. Motivation as a factor in the acquisition of new responses. In *Current Theory and Research in Motivation: A Symposium*. Lincoln: University of Nebraska, 1953, pp. 24-49.

Harlow, H. F. & Harlow, Margaret K. Social deprivation in monkeys. *Scientific American*, 1962, *207*, 136-146.

Helson, H. (Ed.) *Theoretical Foundations of Psychology*. New York: D. Van Nostrand Co., 1951.

Hill, L. B. *Psychotherapeutic Intervention in Schizophrenia*. Chicago: University of Chicago, 1955.

Hobbs, N. Group-centered psychotherapy. In C .R. Rogers, *Client-centered Therapy: Its Current Practice, Implications and Theory*. Boston: Houghton Mifflin, 1951, pp. 278-319.

Hollon, T. H. Ego psychology and the supportive therapy of borderline states. *Psychotherapy*, 1966, *3*, 135-138.

Horney, Karen. *The Neurotic Personality of Our Time*. New York: W. W. Norton & Co., 1937.

Hull, C. L. *Principles of Behavior: An Introduction to Behavior Theory*. New York: Appleton-Century-Crofts, 1943.

Jacobson, E. *Progressive Relaxation,* (2nd ed.) Chicago: University Chicago Press, 1938.

Jahoda, Marie. *Current Concepts of Positive Mental Health.* New York: Basic Books, 1958.

Klapman, J. W. *Group Psychotherapy: Theory and Practice.* New York: Grune & Stratton, 1959.

Klapman, J. W. The case for didactic group psychotherapy. In M. Rosenbaum & M. Berger (Eds.), *Group Psychotherapy and Group Function.* New York: Basic Books, 1963, pp. 328-339, (orig. pub. 1950).

Krasner, L. Behavior modification research and the role of the therapist. In L. A. Gottschalk & H. Auerback (Eds.), *Methods of Research in Psychotherapy.* New York: Meredith Publishing, 1966, pp. 292-305.

Loevinger, Jane. The meaning and measurement of ego development. *American Psychologist,* 1966, *21,* 195-206.

McReynolds, P. Anxiety, perception, and schizophrenia. In D. D. Jackson (Ed.), *The Etiology of Schizophrenia.* New York: Basic Books, 1960, pp. 248-294.

Malone, T. P. An operational definition of schizophrenia. In J. G. Dawson, et al. (Eds.), *Psychotherapy with Schizophrenics: A Reappraisal.* Baton Rouge: Louisiana State University, 1961, pp. 123-135.

Marks, I. M., et al. Common ground between behavior therapy and psychodynamic methods. *Brit. J. Med. Psychol.,* 1966, *39,* 11-23.

Marsh, L. C. Group therapy and the psychiatric clinic. In M. Rosenbaum & M. Berger (Eds.), *Group Psychotherapy and Group Function.* New York: Basic Books, 1963, pp. 131-142, (orig. pub. 1935).

Marx, M. H. (Ed.) *Psychological Theory.* New York: The Macmillan Co., 1951.

Monroe, R. R. Psychotherapy as a adjunctive treatment for schizophrenia. In J. G. Dawson, et al. (Eds.), *Psychotherapy with Schizophrenics: A Reappraisal.* Baton Rouge: Louisiana State University, 1961, pp. 25-45.

Munroe, Ruth L. *Schools of Psychoanalytic Thought: An Exposition, Critique, and Attempt at Integration.* New York: Dryden Press, 1955.

Murphy, G. Group psychotherapy in our society. In M. Rosenbaum & M. Berger (Eds.), *Group Psychotherapy and Group Function.* New York: Basic Books, 1963, pp. 33-41, (orig. speech 1960).

Neighbor, J. E. et al. An approach to the selection of patients for group psychotherapy. In M. Rosenbaum & M. Berger (Eds.), *Group Psychotherapy and Group Function.* New York: Basic Books, 1963, pp. 413-423, (orig. pub. 1958).

Nissen, H. W. The nature of the drive as innate determinant of behavioral organization. In M. R. Jones (Ed.), *Nebraska Symposium on Motivation.* Lincoln: University of Nebraska, 1954, pp. 281-321.

Perry, J. W. Image, complex, and transference in schizophrenia. In A. Burton (Ed.), *Psychotherapy of the Psychoses.* New York: Basic Books, 1961, pp. 90-123.

Pious, W. L. A hypothesis about the nature of schizophrenic behavior. In A. Burton (Ed.), *Psychotherapy of the Psychoses*. New York: Basic Books, 1961, pp. 43-68.

Powdermaker, Florence, et al. *Group Psychotherapy Studies in Methodology of Research and Therapy*. Cambridge: Harvard University, 1953.

Preston, M. G. Methodological considerations. In H. Helson (Ed.), *Theoretical Foundations of Psychology*. New York: D. Van Nostrand Co., 1951, pp. 1-46.

Rachman, S. The current status of behavior therapy. *Arch. Gen. Psychiat.* 1965, *13*, 418-423.

Roessler, R. The therapist's feelings in psychotherapy with schizophrenics. In J. G. Dawson, et al. (Eds.), *Psychotherapy with Schizophrenics: A Reappraisal*. Baton Rouge: Louisiana State University, 1961, pp. 107-117.

Rogers, C. R. *Counseling and Psychotherapy*. Boston: Houghton Mifflin, 1942.

Rogers, C. R. *Client-centered Therapy: Its Current Practice, Implications and Theory*. Boston: Houghton Mifflin, 1951.

Rogers, C. R. A process conception of psychotherapy. *American Psychologist*, 1958, *13*, 142-149.

Rogers, C. R. A theory of psychotherapy with schizophrenics and a proposal for its empirical investigation. In J. G. Dawson, et al. (Eds.), *Psychotherapy with Schizophrenics: A Reappraisal*. Baton Rouge: Louisiana State University, 1961, pp. 3-19.

Rose, S. Horney concepts in group psychotherapy. In M. Rosenbaum & M. Berger (Eds.), *Group Psychotherapy and Group Function*. New York: Basic Books, 1963, pp. 195-203, (orig. pub. 1957).

Rosen, J. N. *Direct Analysis*. New York: Grune & Stratton, 1953.

Rosen, J. N. *Psychoanalysis Direct and Indirect*. Doylestown, Pa.: The Doylestown Foundation, 1964.

Rosenbaum, M. Group psychotherapy and psychodrama. In B. B. Wolman (Ed.), *Handbook of Clinical Psychology*. New York: McGraw-Hill, 1965, pp. 1254-1274.

Rosenbaum, M. & Berger, M. (Eds.) *Group Psychotherapy and Group Function*. New York: Basic Books, 1963.

Ruesch, J. Non-verbal language in therapy. *Psychiatry*, 1955, *18*, 323-330.

Ruesch, J. & Bateson, G. *Communication: The Social Matrix of Psychiatry*. New York: Norton & Co., 1951.

Ruesch, J. & Kees, W. *Nonverbal Communication: Notes on the Visual Perception of Human Relations*. Los Angeles: University of California, 1956.

Scheflen, A. E. Fostering introjection as a psychotherapeutic technique in schizophrenia. In J. G. Dawson, et al. (Eds.), *Psychotherapy with Schizophrenics: A Reappraisal*. Baton Rouge: Louisiana University, 1961, pp. 79-97.

Schilder, P. Results and problems of group psychotherapy in severe neuroses. In M. Rosenbaum & M. Berger (Eds.), *Group Psychotherapy and Group Function*. New York: Basic Books, 1963, pp. 218-227, (orig. pub. 1939).

Schlien, J. M. A client-centered approach to schizophrenia: First approximation. In A. Burton (Ed.), *Psychotherapy of the Psychoses.* New York: Basic Books, 1961, pp. 285-329.

Searles, H. F. *Collected Papers on Schizophrenia and Related Subjects.* New York: International Universities Press, 1965, (orig. pub. 1951-1964).

Sechekaye, Marguerite A. *New Psychotherapy in Schizophrenia.* Transl. G. Ruben-Rabson. New York: Grune & Stratton, 1956.

Sechekaye, Marguerite A. Introduction. In A. Burton (Ed.), *Psychotherapy of the Psychoses.* New York: Basic Books, 1961.

Secord, P. F. & Backman, C. W. Personality theory and the problem of stability and change in individual behavior: An interpersonal approach. *Psychol. Rev.,* 1961, *68,* 21-32.

Skinner, B. F. *The Behavior of Organisms.* New York: Appleton-Century-Crofts, 1938.

Skinner, B. F. *Science and Human Behavior.* New York: The Macmillan Co., 1953.

Skinner, B. F. *Verbal Behavior.* New York: Appleton-Century-Crofts, 1957.

Slavson, S. R. Group therapy special section meeting. In M. Rosenbaum & Berger (Eds.), *Group Psychotherapy and Group Function.* New York: Basic Books, 1963, pp. 228-241, (orig. pub. 1943).

Smolen, E. M. & Lifton, N. A special treatment program for schizophrenic children in a child guidance clinic. *Am. J. of Orthopsychiatry,* 1966, *36,* 736-742.

Speers, R. W. & Lansing, G. *Group Therapy in Childhood Psychosis.* Chapel Hill: University of North Carolina, 1965.

Standish, C. T. & Semard, E. V. Group psychotherapy with psychotics. In M. Rosenbaum & M. Berger (Eds.), *Group Psychotherapy and Group Function.* New York: Basic Books, 1963, pp. 477-486, (orig. pub. 1951).

Stierlin, H. Individual therapy of schizophrenic patients and hospital structure. In A. Burton (Ed.), *Psychotherapy of the Psychoses.* New York: Basic Books, 1961, pp. 329-348.

Sullivan, H. S. *The Interpersonal Theory of Psychiatry.* New York: W. W. Norton & Co., 1953.

Sullivan, H. S. *The Psychiatric Interview.* New York: W. W. Norton & Co., 1954.

Sullivan, H. S. *Clinical Studies in Psychiatry.* New York: W. W. Norton & Co., 1956.

Tate, G. T. An experimental study of two aspects of schizophrenic interpersonal relationships. Unpublished doctoral dissertation. Lexington: University of Kentucky, 1957.

Tolman, E. C. The intervening variable. In M. H. Marx (Ed.), *Psychological Theory.* New York: The Macmillan Co., 1951, pp. 87-102, (orig. pub. 1936).

Tuddenham, R. D. Jean Piaget and the world of the child. *American Psychologist,* 1966, *21,* 207-217.

Ulman, L. & Krasner, L. (Eds.) *Case Studies in Behavior Modification.* New York: Holt, Rinehart and Winston, 1965.

Ulman, L. & Krasner, L. (Eds.) *Research in Behavior Modification.* New York: Holt, Rinehart and Winston, 1966.

Wallace, A. F. C. & Fogelson, R. D. The identity struggle. In I. Boszormeny-nagy & J. L. Framo (Eds.), *Intensive Family Therapy: Theoretical and Practical Aspects.* New York: Harper & Row, 1965, pp. 365-406.

Weakland, J. H. The "double-bind" hypothesis of schizophrenia and three-party interaction. In D. D. Jackson (Ed.), *The Etiology of Schizophrenia.* New York: Basic Books, 1960, pp. 373-388.

Whitaker, C. A., *et al.* Countertransference in the family treatment of schizophrenia. In *Intensive Family Therapy: Theoretical and Practical Aspects.* New York: Harper & Row, 1965, pp. 323-342.

Will, O. A. Process, psychotherapy, and schizophrenia. In A. Burton (Ed.), *Psychotherapy of the Psychoses.* New York: Basic Books, 1961, pp. 10-42.

Winder, C. L. Some psychological studies of schizophrenics. In D. D. Jackson (Ed.), *The Etiology of Schizophrenia.* New York: Basic Books, 1960, pp. 191-247.

Wolman, B. B. Schizophrenia and related disorders. In B. B. Wolman (Ed.), *Handbook of Clinical Psychology.* New York: McGraw Hill, 1965, pp. 976-1029.

Wolman, B. B. Interactional psychotherapy with schizophrenics. *Psychotherapy,* 1966, *3,* 61-70.

Wolpe, J. *Psychotherapy by Reciprocal Inhibition.* Stanford: Standford University, 1958.

Wynne, L. C. *et al.* Pseudo-mutuality in the family relations in schizophrenics. *Psychiatry,* 1958, *21,* 205-220.

Young, P. T. *Motivation and Emotion: A Survey of the Determinants of Human and Animal Activity.* New York: Wiley & Sons, 1961.

Index